PRAIS
DR. ROSEANI

MW00984304

"My friend RoseAnne Coleman is a great story teller. She enchants readers with her real-life stories that teach subtle truths about God, life, and relationships. In this charming book, you will find story gems told by one who knows the truth of 'to get where you are going you need to know where you come from.' I laughed, cried, nodded in agreement, and remembered my own stories. Buy it, read it, and buy another copy for a special friend as a delightful gift. I will."

— Ruth Graham, Author of *In Every Pew Sits a Broken Heart: Hope for the Hurting.* Daughter of Ruth and Billy Graham

"A compelling aroma wafts through these delicious stories that will whet your hunger for heaven. My life couldn't have been more different from a southern girl growing up in a pastor's home, yet the stories bring our universal struggles, dreams, and desires to the surface and train our appetite for what we are most meant to desire: the goodness of God. These brilliantly written stories will draw you to the wonder of what we all are most meant to become as truly human, truly alive, and simply true."

— Dan B. Allender, Ph.D., President and Professor of Counseling Psychology Mars Hill Graduate School, Author, *The Wounded Heart*; *Leading with a Limp*; *To be Told*

"RoseAnne Coleman's *The Stories I Keep* is as charming and as deliciously Southern as her own name is. Beyond the charm and the regional appeal, however, there is an intimacy with Jesus and a candor about the relationship between Him and her that would make any Christian want to read and remember these stories."

— Phyllis Tickle, Author and Founding Editor, *Publishers Weekly* Religion Department

"In John 15, Jesus says that as we live in His Father's garden and abide in Him like a branch abides in a vine, we will bear fruit and be full of joy. RoseAnne Coleman is a 'John 15 woman!' Every week she invites hundreds of women to take a stroll with her through Her Father's Garden as she shares stories of how He is at work growing, pruning, fertilizing and tilling the soil of their lives. This book contains many of those stories that will encourage you to abide with the One who offers abundant joy and fruit that remains."

— Jeff Helton, Teaching Pastor at Fellowship Bible Church, Brentwood, Tennessee

PRAISE FOR
DR. ROSEANNE COLEMAN

"*The Stories I Keep* is a perfect title for RoseAnne's book. Stories are treasures, and when told well, can bring about real change in a person's heart and life. RoseAnne is gifted at not only telling stories well but also inviting the reader to step inside her memories for a journey you won't forget. I am honored to call her friend, and I will always treasure her stories."

— Denise Jones, Singer, Point of Grace

"RoseAnne Coleman is a wildly funny, biblically deep, totally energized servant of the King of Kings! If you are looking for an author who effectively conveys truth to a postmodern audience, RoseAnne is ideal."

— Carol Kent, Author of *A New Kind of Normal* and *When I Lay My Isaac Down* and Speaker, Women of Faith

"RoseAnne is one-of-a-kind! The real deal! And, it comes through in this treasure-chest of stories! I've grown under her incredible teaching and mentoring, co-labored with her in ministry at our church in Brentwood, Tennessee, and now, gleaned from her depth and humor in *The Stories I Keep*. Each chapter encouraged me to ponder my own life's stories, helping me to be even more thankful for the path and relationships in which He's directed me. There is wisdom weaved into each story from the voice of a master teacher. I know RoseAnne to be true, loving, purposeful and all about what the Father leads her in - one being the writing of this book!"

— Melinda Seibert, Director of Women's Ministries (2004-2008), Fellowship Bible Church, Brentwood, Tennessee, Former Dallas Cowboys Cheerleader (1981-1984)

THE STORIES I KEEP

Dr. RoseAnne Coleman

XYZZY PRESS

For information about permission to reproduce selections from this book, write to Permissions, Xyzzy Press, 9105 Concord Hunt Circle, Brentwood, TN 37027

Unless noted, scripture quotations are taken from The King James Version.

Scripture quotations marked (AMP) are taken from the Amplified® Bible, Copyright © 1954, 1958, 1962, 1964, 1965, 1987 by The Lockman Foundation. Used by permission. (www.Lockman.org)

Scripture quotations marked (ESV) are from The Holy Bible, English Standard Version®, copyright © 2001 by Crossway Bibles, a publishing ministry of Good News Publishers. Used by permission. All rights reserved.

Scripture quotations marked (NASB) are taken from the New American Standard Bible®, Copyright © 1960, 1962, 1963, 1968, 1971, 1972, 1973, 1975, 1977, 1995 by The Lockman Foundation. Used by permission. (www.Lockman.org)

Cover & Interior Design: **Birdsong Creative, Inc.**, Franklin, TN
www.birdsongcreative.com

Library of Congress Cataloging-in-Publication Data

Coleman, RoseAnne.
  The stories I keep / by RoseAnne Coleman.
    p. cm.
  Summary: "Life lessons from the author's experiences"--Provided by publisher.
  ISBN-13: 978-1-60148-007-1 (tradepaper)
  ISBN-10: 1-60148-007-5 (tradepaper)
  1. Coleman, RoseAnne. 2. Coleman, RoseAnne—Childhood and youth. 3. Coleman, RoseAnne—Family. 4. Christian biography—Alabama. 5. Children of clergy—Alabama—Biography. 6. Alabama—Biography. 7. Conduct of life. 8. Spiritual life—Baptists. I. Title.
  BR1725.C538A3 2008
  277.3'0825092--dc22
  [B]
                          2008035521

❧ CONTENTS ❧

❧ FOREWORD ❧

When I began this book, I planned something totally different from what came. And I find that humorous, because my life has been this way, too, with events not sticking to my schedule, with my path not leading to where I first thought I would go. What came were stories of my childhood, stories of people I admired, stories of laughter and tears, stories of inspiration and instruction.

This is not a Bible study—although that is what I do on an almost daily basis. God knows there are enough of those, and any local bookstore can satisfy that need. Evidently God had a different plan for me—big surprise. I realized He wanted me to focus on stories, not lessons, on learning as opposed to teaching. As I thought about it, the common denominator of everyone's life is story, unique to an individual but common to humankind.

STORIES WORTH TELLING

In the South of the past, the summer temperatures, increased by the heat of the cooking stoves, drove folks out of their houses and onto their porches. No matter the social class or bank account, everyone was hot. Outside, amidst the music of katydids and crickets, the conversation and storytelling were the sweet desserts served after dinner, oftentimes the richest fare of the night.

Today there is very little such sitting around with neighbors or friends. Air conditioning makes the indoors very comfortable, life is moving faster, and modern conveniences like computers and Black-Berries make it too easy to just keep "doing." Thankfully, though, if you look for them, you can still find opportunities—on a walk with a friend or during the car ride home from a soccer game—to share a story, recount experiences, or pass along lessons learned.

Even with the busyness of life and the fading of traditional forums for storytelling, I am confident that the stories are there and that they will not go away. In fact, the stories play over and over in your mind because they happened to you, didn't they? Choosing to tell the stories may increase their beauty or intensify their sting, but one thing is certain: the stories are kept. They remain.

STORIES WITHIN A STORY

What follows are some of my stories—some that have caused great delight as well as brought life-threatening pain. As I tell these stories for myself one more time, as I share them with others, and as I write them for you, I begin to see more clearly than ever the greater story that God has been writing in my life all along.

I also experience once again how stories can be life giving, and I better understand why God commanded the Israelites to tell of His faithfulness from generation to generation. It is in the telling of both His story and our own stories that He brings to the foreground the jewels—the lessons, the moments of life worth really keeping— and puts aside that to which we need not cling.

So I hope these stories encourage you to revisit the ones that you have kept and to share what you find worthwhile. As you tell yours, encourage others to tell theirs. Undoubtly, some discoveries await. Who knows the treasures you will find?

Dr. RoseAnne Coleman
Rose Hill, Tennessee
September 17, 2008

A TALE OF PEAS

by Karen Ann Fentress

Awed by the rich color of each pod,
my fingers awkwardly split the seams
as dried, damp or very moist peas
emerged in surprising hues and patterns.
As we shelled, we mused on story,
the cadence of voices, the lilt and
metre of *uh-huh*, *yes'm*, and *that's right*.

I reckon to myself stories are like
the fruit of the dirt we hold and release:

Some come out ready, popping across
the porch floor and bounce toward
eternity; others are dried, past life, past
even the third day so that only hope
of a long soak on the stove-top can
bring them to their fullness. Even the
ripe, damp ones who sit straight in the
husk and make no fuss about falling into
the bowl, do not tire invested
listeners with their accounts of birth,
freedom, life and death.

So it is with the yarns spun on porches
across our land: as we listen we might
learn a thing or two, waiting on a plot to
unfold.

CHAPTER 1

THE STORY OF ME

I have always loved the land. Even as a child I took great pleasure in seeing a pasture or a garden, because farming is in my blood. My mother's people grew vegetables and beautiful flowers. They learned by observing and working with immediate and extended family members who gardened and farmed, all feeding their families with the food they grew and the animals they raised.

However, my life's path led to academics, not agriculture, until I moved to an acre and a half of land in a rural area where there are still open spaces. And I have discovered an ability to care for growing things, a great surprise because my houseplants historically died a cruel death. Instead of being a plant killer, I saw my real self: a modern woman who never took the time to care for much of anything—including herself.

"HOW HARD CAN THIS BE?"

When I decided to have a garden, I rented a Kubota tractor, a bottom plow, and a box tiller from Terry at TJ Rentals. He showed me how to work all the equipment and then encouraged me not to be afraid, but to have fun. This was not the first time Terry had been my coach and cheerleader. A year earlier I had rented a backhoe, and Terry himself had come out to Rose Hill, my home, to teach me how to use the big machine.

As the tractor inched along in its lowest gear so the plow could best do its work, I looked back periodically to see the implement cut deep into the earth. As I smelled the fresh-turned dirt, memories of my grandmother and her garden welled up in my heart. It was as if I had come full circle, and I felt more centered and peaceful—and tired and sore—than I had in many years; it was as if I were returning to the home place where I belonged.

I learned as I went and made many mistakes along the way. My rows were *mostly* straight, and I remember a certain Sunday morning when I took my cup of coffee to the garden to admire the knee-high corn after a summer's rain. As I got closer to the garden, the corn was not where it was supposed to be. I ran the rest of the way, just to discover that the blessed rain had beaten down my new corn until most of it was lying on the ground instead of standing tall with new growth. I dumped my coffee in the grass and spent the rest of the morning pulling each stalk upright and packing more dirt around the base for stability.

It was my first lesson in what all the old-timers know: every passing moment holds another opportunity for something to go wrong in the garden. If not bugs, it's plant-decimating animals; if not drought, it's rains that dislodge roots and beat down tender growth; if not one thing, it's another. And it became very clear to me why, when small farms were abundant, America was known as a praying nation. After all, only God brings rain, and people knew they must pray for God's help. Farming is definitely too big an undertaking for mortals. When rain falls, when seeds germinate, when plants grow, when pests are thwarted, and when the family is fed today and has more to put away for the winter—all that is both an answer to prayer and a call to prayer, to pour out our thanks to God for His mercies.

My first garden produced okra, squash, cantaloupes, corn, and tomatoes. One of my biggest thrills was to pick the vegetables and then take them to the kitchen to either cook or serve immediately. Store-bought vegetables are not even in the same league as homegrown produce coming straight from the field to the table. I was proud to be eating what I had grown, but I was also humbled that God had blessed the work of my hands.

By toiling in the dirt and being outside for hours at a time, I began to see God and His world with new eyes. Discovering the beautiful blossoms of okra and yellow squash, I took pictures of them like a proud parent. I was constantly amazed at God's intricate attention to detail and beauty in the most common of plants. I watched the industriousness of birds. I was stunned to realize that a Carolina wren, with only a miniscule brain, is able to weave thousands of pieces of straw, grass, twigs, horse hair, string, and even strips of plastic into a concave, symmetrical, bowl-shaped nest in which the eggs and then the young fit snugly. The nest's exterior, however, is an asymmetrical shape that the bird secures into the crevices of a tree branch. Wow!

Each year I learned more and my garden grew larger, requiring more time but yielding more produce. Since I'd had some success, I decided one summer to grow and sell vegetables to earn needed money, thinking, "Surely I can do this. How hard can it be?" Just for the record and after the fact, those are the words I will have carved into my gravestone as my cause of death! First, the work required my being outside an average of ten hours a day, preparing beds and planting seeds and plants. One week I dug over twenty holes three feet deep and two feet wide. I have a picture of my standing in one up to my knees. I had never worked so hard—nor been so dirty—in my life.

WHOSE RESPONSIBILITY IS THIS?

Another factor raising the level of difficulty was that Tennessee experienced a drought that resulted in severe water rationing. Also, sixty tomatoes plants in the new field became infested with spider mites. The leaves on the plants curled up and began to die. I used everything anyone told me would kill the little sons of bugs. Nothing worked, and I lost over thirty plants, the money I had invested, any inventory of produce to sell, and many sweat-soaked hours. However, I have since realized that God had another reason for my being a full-time gardener: He wanted me to learn to walk more slowly, to talk less frequently, to listen more often, and to look intently on the world around me.

If God led me to prepare the ground and plant seeds for vegetables and zinnias in order to help me see what I was basing my life on, I would pronounce the experience a complete success. I spent most of the daylight hours in silence, working as my momma's people did for many generations in this very state. I realized there is rhythm in life that nature not only recognizes, but also lives by. Wendell Berry states that his grandfather "lived a life of limits, both suffered and strictly observed, in a world of limits. I learned much of that world from him and others, but then I changed; I entered the world of labor-saving machines and of limitless cheap fossil fuel. It would take me years of reading, thought, and experience to learn again that in this world limits are not only inescapable but indispensible."[1]

To live a life of limits seems to fly in the face of the modern American definition of success. We point to the many inventions that have increased our comfort and lessened our work, so that we live as if we are no longer subject to the same restrictions that our grandparents acknowledged as the inescapable cycle of this revolving orb: sunrise and sunset; light and dark; winter, spring, summer, fall; seeding and harvest. The holy rhythm that has governed and balanced life on earth since Creation is no longer recognized as essential, if it is even recognized at all.

Working in my gardens day after day helped me recognize and appreciate that divine cadence; but instead of trusting and being content with what God ordained, I became more and more anxious as evidence of my hard work began to shrivel and die for lack of water from heaven.

One day I had lunch with my friend Robert who was raised on a farm outside Knoxville, Tennessee. He said something so profound that it was one of those milestones that will forever mark where I had been from where I was going.

Robert pointed out that I was becoming more and more fretful as I realized that the fruit of my labors would not be manifest in tomatoes, watermelon, cantaloupe, cucumbers, squash, purple pod beans, and green pole beans. Of course I was! I was responsible! And how could I be successful if I had no fruit to sell so others would know that I had overcome the odds?

Robert listened to my wailing for a respectable amount of time. Then he looked at me incredulously and said, "You don't think you're responsible for making the vegetables and flowers grow, do you?!"

His question and the way he asked it rocked me back

on my heels. I had taken on God's responsibility in the growing process! In that moment I also realized that by focusing totally on what I produced externally rather than on what was being produced inside me, I was missing the most important crop of all: me, plus character, patience, discovery of God's holy boundaries for my days and nights, an appreciation of the smallest things, and the choice of time to think, reflect, and remember.

All of us need to take the time to prepare the dirt of our hearts for receiving the seeds God sows.

WEEDS, BUGS, AND MANURE

It was only when the heat increased, the rain decreased, and my hope had dwindled to nothing that I began to recognize my self-indulgence, my arrogance, my need to acknowledge that I am a woman who must live within the boundary lines of my life. How did I get so far off the path set so clearly by those who had gone before me? Truthfully, I had much book learning but not much wisdom about living as a created one, not as if I were the Creator.

While hoeing weeds unaffected by the drought, I looked back at my past instead of looking to the future. Remembering the stories of my childhood, I thought about the people who had been in my life, what I had learned from them, what I needed to un-learn, what I still needed to learn. As I acknowledged my poverty of spirit, my soul began to cherish the quiet, and I grew rich in the way Psalm 92:13-14 (AMP) describes:

> Planted in the house of the Lord, they shall flourish ... [Growing in grace] they shall still bring forth fruit in old age; they shall be full ... [of spiritual vitality] and [rich in ... trust, love, and contentment].

Here God says that wealth is measured not in money or possessions, but in the bounty that comes from a life well lived, a life that produces the fruit of a wise heart. How many people—and maybe you're among them—would give all their earthly possessions to be "rich in ... trust, love, and contentment"?

As we walk through the fields of my life, we'll stop to listen to someone's story, to discuss a thought, to listen to the wind, and to watch the birds. Maybe by sundown you will have gathered enough in your basket to eat as well as to plant for your own crops. Possibly you have plenty of seeds to plant, but your soil is poor and needs enriching. That nourishment will come.

You see, I have discovered the proper use of manure as I gardened. Fresh manure will burn plants, killing them instead of promoting growth. However, as manure ages, the composition is altered so that it will enrich the soil and feed the plant, helping it to produce bigger, healthier, and more abundant fruit.

The same is true with the "manure" in your life and mine. Just like manure we use in our gardens, difficulties usually need time before they can enrich us and make wisdom grow without extinguishing the flickering flame within us. You are welcome to borrow some of my nicely aged soil enrichers as I open the compost bin of my stories. But my guess is, you probably have enough "manure" of your own to help you grow—if you will just give it enough time for the stink to go away. Sifting through my past mistakes, sorrows, and disappointments, however, may free you to appreciate your own supply of fertilizer.

Let's not waste anymore time. Daylight's burning.

The Stories I Keep

CHAPTER 2

BROKEN COLORS

Until first grade I was unaware of prejudice, and Momma would tell two stories about my being color-blind. The setting for the first story was Pell City, Alabama. We were eating supper at the home of bank president Pat and Bertalee Robertson. (In the South, we have dinner at noon and supper at night.)

Although I was maybe three years old, I had been allowed to sit with the adults because Mr. Pat and Mrs. (pronounced *Miz*) Bertalee adored me. Momma said that, all of a sudden, the maid came in and asked Mrs. Bertalee what she needed. Surprised, Mrs. Bertalee said she needed nothing. The maid looked confused and pushed back through the swinging door to the kitchen.

In a minute, she returned and again asked what was needed. Upon investigation, the Robertsons realized I was pushing the service button located under the table close to my chair; I had been causing the confusion. To my great delight, I spent the rest of the meal having fun in the kitchen, being entertained by a woman grateful to have the button untouched.

"DO YOU LOVE JESUS?"

The second story Momma would tell revealed my views on race.

When I was four years old, my dad was being considered for the pastorate of the First Baptist Church of Ashville, Alabama, a very small town about an hour northeast of Birmingham. While my dad and momma were at supper with the men of what was called the "pulpit committee" and their wives, I stayed at one of their homes with the maid. When my parents came to collect me, the beautiful, black woman pulled my momma aside and told her of the questions I had asked her:

"Lillie Mae, I love Jesus. Do *you* love Jesus too?"

"I shore do, Miss RoseAnne. Lillie Mae shore do."

"Well, Lillie Mae, you need to come to our church next Sunday!"

"Nome, Miss RoseAnne. Lillie Mae probably won't be comin' to your church next Sunday."

"Why not?" I demanded.

"Well, Miss RoseAnne, I think I better go to my church, and you go to yor'n," she replied.

I stood up in my chair so I could look the black woman in the eyes. "Oh, yes, you can, Lillie Mae," I literally squealed in my delight, "because my daddy told me that everyone who loves Jesus needs to be coming to our church, and you said that you loved Jesus, so that means you and all your family and all your friends who love Jesus need to be at our church!"

Momma thanked the chuckling woman and felt grateful that she had not told the story in front of the committee member's wife who would not have been so thrilled at the prospective pastor's child evangelist. Momma tried to explain to me on the way home that although I had done a good job inviting Lillie Mae, she attended her own church and would want to keep attending it.

At four, I was too young to understand what *segregation* or *prejudice* meant, but two years later when I started to school, I learned my hardest lesson ever—and it had nothing to do with the black or white color of a person's skin. Rather, it involved sixty-two more hues from God's color wheel than just those two.

THE COWBOY WAY

Ashville High School housed first through twelfth grade, and it combined those of us who lived within the city limits and those who lived out in the country and up on the mountain, including many poor farmers who planted tomatoes and other vegetables to sell. Many of the country kids had to help their parents with the crops.

Those children would be absent from school in the fall for

harvest and in the springtime for planting. So, not many passed to their next grade, making them easy prey for the jeers and criticism of students and adults alike. One such girl was in my first-grade class. She was probably eight years old and too big for our pint-sized tables and chairs. I tried to be friends with her because I had experienced teasing and being made fun of. (Besides, I was bound by Rule #4 of the Roy Rogers Riders Club: "Protect the weak and help them.")

I don't remember her name, so I'll call her Shelia. I do, however, remember her wandering eye, a physical trait that made her the object of even more scorn from those who had straight eyes but blind hearts.

It was 1961, the first year our school began serving hot lunches. However, Olice and Brady Machen had given me a vinyl Roy Rogers lunch box when I started school, so I wanted to take my lunch. In between the two first-grade rooms was a coatroom where we stored our lunches and milk money until we marched to the cafeteria.

Every Saturday I would get up early to I could watch my hero, Roy Rogers, and his faithful horse, Trigger. I could almost quote the Roy Rogers Riders Club Rules with Roy, and I had pledged to right wrong wherever I could. So, I was excited to carry my new lunch box as a daily reminder of my hero and my purpose in life.

However, as I opened the box on the first day of school, I found an egg salad sandwich instead of my expected peanut butter and banana! Unsettled, I looked up to see more confused faces, and some of the girls began to cry. I didn't cry—for that wasn't the Cowboy Way—but I was upset.

Can you imagine a table full of six-year-olds, distraught and confused, crying for the sandwiches their mothers had made? The two teachers quickly realized that someone had played a prank on us, and with the soothing way of veteran first-grade teachers, they somehow calmed us down at the same time that they matched sandwich to child. When I finally began to eat, though, I saw that the girl with the wandering eye didn't have a lunch. She was just sitting at the table with no food. Not even a carton of milk.

"What would Roy do?" I thought, looking at his image on my thermos. (At that time, Roy came to my mind more often than Jesus. I also liked the boots, hats, and guns that made me look like a real cowgirl. I didn't really like the sandals or long robes that I saw in the Bible illustrations in our Sunday school room.) I picked up half of my sandwich and asked Shelia, "Would you like half of my sandwich? I'm not gonna eat all of it."

She looked embarrassed, but nodded her head and reached for the offered half. But before I could complete my good deed, our teacher grabbed her arm and said, "No, Shelia! You need to bring your own food, and, RoseAnne, I'm sure your momma would want you to finish what she made for you."

The teacher's raised voice got the attention of the whole table, embarrassing Shelia and me in front of everyone else. It was common for me to be in trouble for no good reason and punished in front of other people, so I was familiar with shame. I just didn't think I would experience that at school.

A THUNDER CRACK

When we returned to our classroom, we started our lessons, and I forgot all about the sandwich incident. It came time to color a picture our teacher had handed out. As with my Roy Rogers' lunch box, I was excited because I had a brand-new box of crayons—and it was the twenty-four-count box! When I looked up after working a little while, Shelia was just sitting with no crayons.

"You better get out your colors," I whispered.

"Ain't got none," she whispered back.

"Here! We can share."

Shelia looked down at my crayon box and softly murmured, "Thank you." She didn't look up, and I was slightly relieved. Even though I didn't think Shelia's wandering eye was the mark of the devil like a classmate's momma had said, it was hard talking to Shelia because I never knew if I should look at the moving eye or stay with the other one.

This girl who was repeating first grade for at least the third time took one of the colors and held it in her hand, real gently, like she was holding gold.

All of a sudden, like a thunder crack, the teacher called from the other side of the room, "Shelia, are you stealing RoseAnne's crayons?!" The poor girl dropped the color and pulled her hand back as if she had been shocked by electricity.

Slightly panicked, I answered since Shelia didn't. "Oh no, ma'am! I was just sharing 'cause she doesn't have any colors of her own."

By that time, the teacher was towering over us. "RoseAnne, you just use your colors," she replied as she pushed all my materials back toward me. "Shelia should bring her own, just like everybody else has to do. Shelia, tell your mother again to buy you the required school supplies. You think she would know what you needed by this time!"

I could not believe it. It was my first day of school, and I had already been in trouble twice—both times because of Shelia.

IN TROUBLE AGAIN

When I got home, I waited for Momma to return from her school in Odenville, about thirty minutes from Ashville. I heard the slam of the back-porch screen door, and I met her in the kitchen.

"Momma, I need some more colors for school tomorrow. Can we go right now to Mr. Newman's drugstore and get them?"

"Why, RoseAnne, I just bought you a box of twenty-four! What's wrong with them?" my mother asked as she walked to the dining room table to relieve her arms of the books and the stacks of papers that had to be graded by morning.

I didn't notice how tired she looked, so I stayed the course: "Well, I still have them, but other kids have that box with sixty-four, including 'copper' and 'flesh' and a sharpener in the back. I think I really need the bigger box for my schoolwork."

My mother, Melrose Bibles Coleman, was just twenty-six years old herself, with a six-year-old, a one-year-old, a full-time teaching job, and a busy husband. Also, in those days, the pastor's salary hired the whole family. So Momma also worked as the church's pianist, organist, nursery organizer, children's choir director, vacation Bible school director, and any other volunteer position that needed filling.

My momma had to work outside the home to help with the family bills, and she stretched every dollar. To her credit, I never knew we were poor until we weren't. Since Momma worked, she was fortunate to be able to hire Lillie Mae, the black woman I had invited to church two years before, to come take care of my baby sister, Sherry, during school hours.

Frustrated with my seeming ungratefulness for what I had, Momma said, "Young lady, I don't care what anyone else has! You are going to use the crayons you have until they are all broken. Do you understand me?"

I mumbled, "Yes, ma'am" and went out on the front porch.

I loved that front porch even though my dad said I shouldn't sit there because it was just too dangerous. We lived near a street that everyone had to turn on to get through town, and the eighteen-wheelers didn't slow down much to make the turn. Dad said that "one of these days" a truck was going to take the turn too fast and come crashing through the porch into the living room and den—killing us all.

Made even more attractive by this possibility of danger, the porch was one of my favorite places to be. Alone there, I was free to imagine I was on a ship or a wagon or a stagecoach or in the saddle riding the plains with Roy Rogers and Trigger. When the truck drivers looked my way, I would make an up-and-down motion with my arm, asking them to blow their air horn for me—which most of them did with a smile. It never occurred to me that distracting them as they began their turn might be dangerous. I simply loved the attention and having the horn blown just for me.

That day, while sitting on the front wall of the porch, I thought about what Momma had said and how my first plan had not worked. In fact, I was in trouble again for the third time that day just because I was trying to help the girl who was too large for her chair, whose knees were too high to go under the table.

Still, I knew I had to do something to help Shelia. It wasn't her fault her parents grew tomatoes and she had to plant and pick, just like it wasn't my fault that I had to fold bulletins on Saturday nights, ring the bell on Sunday mornings, go to the sparsely attended church service on Sunday nights when *The Wonderful World of Disney* aired on television, or be at all the adult meetings during the week because I was considered too young to stay alone in our house just across the gravel driveway.

A NEW PLAN

The next day Shelia again didn't bring a lunch or colors to school. By the time I went home that afternoon, though, I had a plan. I was waiting when Momma stepped through the back-porch door into the kitchen.

"Momma, look what happened!" I exclaimed, holding up my hands. "I dropped my box of colors on the front porch, and every one of them broke! I guess I need a new box now."

Momma looked at me and at the broken wax pieces in my cupped, six-year-old hands—that smelled distinctly of crayons.

"Well," she said slowly as she put down her load, "what should we do with these broken ones?"

I bet it was comical as I scrunched up my face as if I were deep in thought and then announced, "I know, Momma! There is this girl in my class who is poor and doesn't have colors, and we get in trouble when we try to share, so maybe we could give these to her!"

Of course, it didn't occur to me to give Shelia the new crayons. I had only been staying awake during church for about a year, so I wasn't aware that our Lord Jesus Christ said that we should do unto others as we would have them do unto us. Furthermore, I didn't see that practiced too much in my world anyway, so I was not familiar with the give-her-the-new-box-to-make-Jesus-happy-but-yourself-sad decision anyway. Besides, Roy had never had a show on sharing crayons, so my conscience was clear.

After looking at me for a moment, Momma asked Lillie Mae if she could stay awhile longer while we walked the two blocks to Newman's Rexall Drugs. On the way Momma made conversation, first asking me about school, finally drawing out my concerns about Shelia's not having any lunch to eat and my teacher's not letting me treat the girl like Roy Rogers or Jesus wanted me to, and then hearing that my teacher scolded us and was mean to Shelia. I bet Momma didn't tell my dad that I was following a cowboy, not a Carpenter, and quoting his rules for living instead of Bible verses. (For the record, Jesus finally caught up with and then passed Roy, but not for a long time.)

That evening when I was trying out every color of the

sixty-four in my new box with the sharpener in the back, I heard Momma on the phone with Mrs. Smith, my friend Rusty's mom. I loved going to Rusty's house because they had ice-cold spring water coming into their house instead of the city water we had.

AN ALMOST MIRACULOUS STORY

Much happened in my small world the next day. Rusty's mom and mine started paying for Shelia to have a hot lunch every day. I gave Shelia her first box of her own crayons, albeit each one was broken in half. She didn't seem to mind, saying that gave her forty-eight instead of the original twenty-four. Finally, I was moved from the mean teacher's class to Mrs. Bell's room on the other side of the first-grade building.

About a month after I moved to the new class, Shelia didn't come out at recess, and no one knew where she had gone. A couple weeks later, my family was on the way to Gadsden to eat at a restaurant. As Dad drove the winding road, we came upon an old pickup truck with a girl standing in the bed right behind the rounded cab. As we drew even with the cab, I realized the girl was Shelia. Her hair was whipping all around her face, and she was smiling.

This would be a miraculous story if Shelia had waved with one hand and held up one of the broken crayons in the other as we passed—but she didn't. As a matter of fact, she didn't even see me because her eyes were closed. In my mind's eye, though, I saw wings unfurl from behind Shelia, and as we went past, I imagined her flying right out of that rusty truck, leaving behind tomatoes and hunger and shame—and a used box of broken colors.

Fly away, Little Bird. Fly far, far away.

The Stories I Keep

Be merciful, just as your Father is merciful.
Do not judge, and you will not be judged;
and do not condemn, and you will not be condemned;
pardon, and you will be pardoned.
Give, and it will be given to you.
They will pour into your lap a good measure—
pressed down, shaken together, and running over.
For by your standard of measure
it will be measured to you in return.

– Jesus in Luke 6:36-38 (NASB)

The Stories I Keep

CHAPTER 3

ROY ROGERS IS
MY HERO

Roy Rogers has always been one of my heroes. Every summer, in fact, I begged my dad to plan a trip to California to visit the Double R Bar Ranch. Dad kept saying, "RoseAnne, you act like we could just pull into his driveway, say, 'Howdy, pardner,' and have Roy invite us in." And I really did believe that the King of the Cowboys would not only welcome us but probably ask us to stay with his family.

Early on Saturday mornings, I would be right in front of the television set in the little room Momma called the "den." For the next two hours, until I couldn't stand to be indoors any longer, I would watch Westerns. There were almost always shows with Roy Rogers and the Sons of the Pioneers, and then later there were shows with Roy Rogers and Dale Evans, who became his wife. At the beginning of every one of the many episodes of *The Roy Rogers Show*, my hero always said the following prayer—and his horse Trigger would close his eyes:

> O Lord, I reckon I'm not much just by myself.
> I fail to do a lot of the things I ought to do.
> But, Lord, when the trails are steep and the passes high,
> Help me to ride it straight the whole way through.

And when in the falling dusk I get the final call,
I do not care how many flowers they send.
Above all else the happiest trail would be
For You to say to me, "Let's ride, My friend."
Amen.[1]

As a preacher's kid, I heard prayers from many people, mostly men. I don't think women prayed aloud in services in the early sixties, although they did many other jobs that kept the church running smoothly. However, some men who were called upon to lead us in a word of prayer did not listen to those specific instructions. Instead of offering a word or two, certain men prayed so many words that it made us kids wonder how long it had been since those guys had talked to God. It was especially bad when these marathon pray-ers were supposed to close a service. On Sunday mornings, all the children were starving, and on Sunday nights, we were ready to go home to catch the last minutes of Walt Disney, *Bonanza*, or *Gunsmoke*.

When Roy prayed his prayer, it was short and to the point. He was showing his viewers that praying to God was the right thing to do and that even a horse could close its eyes in reverence. I do miss that reverence in this modern world; it seems we have explained away, taken away, or shoved away most of what Americans had honored throughout most of our country's existence.

The last thing Roy would do, and I think Dale would join him for this, was ask all the viewers to recite the Roy Rogers Riders Club Rules:

1. Be neat and clean.
2. Be courteous and polite.
3. Always obey your parents.
4. Protect the weak and help them.
5. Be brave but never take chances.
6. Study hard and learn all you can.
7. Be kind to animals and take care of them.
8. Eat all your food and never waste any.
9. Love God and go to Sunday school regularly.
10. Always respect our flag and our country.[2]

After reciting these rules at the end of a show, I was rip-roaring ready to get my hat and guns and hit the trail to do good; I was raring to help anyone in distress. On Saturday morning, the boundary lines of life were clear, and there was no question whether the wrongdoers would be exposed and punished by the strong, who were also kind. Power was held as a sacred trust and exercised with honor.

But I was living my actual life outside the safe place that was defined by Roy's prayer and his rules, so as much as possible I escaped to his world. When I dismounted my trusty steed, and the cactus and boulders of the plains turned back into the familiar grass and trees of the backyard, I always had the slight glimmer of hope that the real world would have somehow gotten better. Then, when I realized all too quickly that things were still the same, I would cinch my gun belt a little tighter and look forward to riding the range with Roy again.

IT MATTERED!

Every Christmas until I was in my twenties or so, I asked for a Roy Rogers cowboy hat. And every Christmas I received a Benny Carle cowboy hat. Benny had a daily afternoon program on WBRC-Channel 6, in Birmingham, Alabama. Maybe my parents thought that it really didn't matter or that I wouldn't notice whose name was on the front just as long as Santa brought me a cowboy hat. Maybe they thought I would be overjoyed to receive *anything* since we didn't have much money.

But, first of all, it did matter—and it mattered a lot—whose name was on the front of the hat. Benny wasn't even a *real* cowboy. He was just a man who dressed up for a kids' show. Benny didn't have a horse, or he would have had it on the show—and even if he'd had a horse, no horse would be able to "turn on a dime and leave you change," as Roy said Trigger did.

Second, having Roy's name on my hat when I rode the living room chair as my horse would make me feel like we were riding together, like I was part of his posse. It was so embarrassing to think about if I ever really did have to confront bad guys: I was sure they would smirk, "Hey, pardner, who is Benny Carle?"

Third, since it did matter whose name was on the front of the hat, I could not hide my disappointment when I didn't see

Roy's name. I guess it did seem that I was ungrateful, because I had received 50 percent of my request. It was a cowboy hat, but my parents did not understand this fact: How could I be bold and proud while fighting the bad guys, righting the wrongs, and saving people in distress if I were wearing the hat of a guy who wasn't even a real cowboy?

A CHRISTMAS I'LL NEVER FORGET

The year I was eight, we had a cowboy Christmas I will never forget.

In the days leading up to Christmas, Momma had asked my two-year-old sister, Sherry, what she wanted for Christmas, and all she would say was "A suck-ker." Obviously, Momma or Dad couldn't wait to tell everyone the unbelievable news: "Have I told you the cutest thing Sherry Lynne says she wants for Christmas?"

In response, a few people asked, "Sherry Lynne just wants a sucker, but what does RoseAnne want?" Evidently I didn't make the cute cut because the answer was "Oh, her list is a little longer and more expensive: a white Roy Rogers cowboy hat, red Roy Rogers boots, and a two-holstered Roy Rogers pistol set." And then there was always laughter, and my eight-year-old face would be as red as a cowboy's bandana. I still held out hope, however, that Santa would ignore my parents' wishes and respond only to the passionate letter I wrote him, explaining my dilemma and, I prayed, persuading him to bring the joy of Roy to at least one Christmas morning.

After hearing the "suck-ker" story several times, I thought back to the day Sherry was brought home from the hospital. I had wanted a little brother and I had made no bones about it, but Momma was one smart woman. When she and the new baby were settled in the bedroom, there was much talk about how great it was going to be to have a little sister who would play cowboy with me. They even took a picture: Sherry is propped up slightly with my cowboy hat behind her head, and I am at her side, holding one of my toy pistols. When I look at the old color photo now, yes, I was smiling, but it's hard to miss where the toy pistol was pointing.

As it tends to do, Christmas morning finally came, and it started out like every other winter morning. There was a process established for rising in our house: I would wake up and then wake

Dad up. I would get back into my warm bed while he lit the gas heaters in each room. Christmas Day was no different, except that Dad was not as grouchy as he usually was when I woke him up not too long after sunrise. Eventually Momma came to get Sherry from her baby bed. I was itching to get into the living room to see what Santa had brought, to see if he had truly understood my cowboy request.

The first thing I saw next to the Christmas tree was a rocking horse connected to a platform by springs. For Sherry. Next to the horse was a pair of red cowboy boots. For Sherry. Then I spotted the red cowboy hat. For Sherry. Momma and Dad were oohing over the baby's Western presents and trying to get her to see them, but the two-year-old was not interested. She was looking for something else. Suddenly, Sherry spied it and started walking as fast as her little legs would go. She headed straight to the doll that had been placed at the back on the Christmas tree—a doll with a sucker in her hand. I can't describe the pandemonium that broke out with Sherry's discovery of the only thing she had asked for and, evidently, the only thing she cared about.

Santa had also left me a black cowboy hat—with "Benny Carle" written on the front. Although there were many presents for me under the tree in the living room that Christmas, I don't remember anything but my black hat and Sherry's horse, boots, hat, and—last but not forgotten—sucker. Momma was the best Santa's helper, and she wouldn't hurt me intentionally. However, since there was so much in my life that was extremely hard, my imagination was my only true way of escape. Roy Rogers didn't only save people in the movies and on television: he would also rescue me.

"HAPPY TRAILS"

I moved on, and eventually Roy Rogers items did not make my Christmas wish list. Things like books and science project kits and board games were more what Santa was asked to bring. I never forgot the King of the Cowboys, but sadly, I learned early that my dreams were silly and would not come true. But there were still twinges whenever I heard *The Wonderful World of Disney* music theme and Jiminy Cricket sang so convincingly that dreams come true when you wish upon a star.

Through education, both in classrooms and from life itself, I learned that—counter to Jiminy's claim—"who you are" evidently does make a difference in whether your dreams come true. So, at a young age, I put away childish things: I retired my Roy Rogers and Trigger saddlebag lunch box, and I resigned myself to eating whatever the lunchroom served. What had I learned? That I was a Benny Carle kid in Alabama.

In 1977 I was a senior at Samford University in Birmingham. My friend Tanya, who lived across the hall in my dorm, was telling me about going home to Brent, a town near Tuscaloosa. When she mentioned that she was going to hear Dale Evans speak, my heart began to pound in my ears, although honestly I never had liked Dale's moving in on Roy's movies. Actually, I was jealous, but I was too young to know what to call the feeling then.

However, I did want to meet Roy Rogers's wife. Tanya warned me that she couldn't promise I would get close enough to meet the celebrity, but we could try. The program was held outside, and as it ended, folks began to push toward the stage in an attempt to meet the writer of "Happy Trails to You," the song that Roy and she sang at the close of each show.

When it looked doubtful that we could make our way to Ms. Evans before she left, Tanya looked at me. "You want to meet her, and I am going to get you up there! Just follow me!" she said in her very Southern accent. She told me to hold on to her blouse and stay right behind her.

I kept practicing quietly what I would say to Dale Evans. I didn't want to repeat the same things I was sure millions of fans worldwide had said to her. I was hoping to be memorable. Tanya "Hello"-ed and "Hey there!"-ed and "Good to see you, too, honey!"-ed our way through the sea of people, and then she said, "Here we are! Now speak to her!" To my surprise, standing right behind the now-older movie star, I was suddenly stricken with fear. Tanya whispered for me to hurry and talk, or else Dale Evans would be gone.

I started to say her name to get her attention, but I had absolutely no voice! My mouth had gone dry, and I could not get a word out. So Tanya took my picture as I stood there, smiling and pointing to Dale's back. I can't remember whether or not she turned around. No matter. I was standing next to the Queen of the Cowboys—who was married to the King.

On the ride home, strangely, for the first time in years, my Benny Carle hat kept coming to mind.

A LITTLE BIT ROCK AND ROLL

Let's fast-forward to 1990. My friend Tricia Walker was the guitar player for a Grand Ole Opry singer. People who performed on the Opry could invite a few guests to each show, and Tricia was kind enough to invite me. She introduced me to Mr. Roy Acuff, and it was gratifying to meet this country music legend.

My first visit backstage at the Opry came soon after I moved to Nashville in 1985. I had never liked the country music I heard over our AM/FM clock radio in the kitchen. I had no idea who Cheryl and Sharon White were, but they were so friendly to me at a prayer meeting I attended that I accepted their invitation to go backstage at the Opry because they were singing with their dad, Buck. My name was placed on "the list" at the back door of the Opryland theater, and upon admittance, I was left to find my way to the stage.

Although I was not the only one with long, permed hair that night, I was the only one wearing the popular style of a white blouse with an upturned collar underneath my dad's old black suit coat with vintage costume jewelry of sparkling crystals pinned on a lapel. I was the last person who would have thought I would own—much less wear—flashy jewelry my momma called "stage jewelry." However, I had won my crystal pin in a drawing at the hair salon that had transformed my straight hair into chemically induced ringlets, thus setting my life on a new, sparkling course. Backstage that night, many were dressed a little bit country in contrast to my rock and roll.

When I asked a lady where I could find The Whites, she said they were on stage. Although they were quite country in style, I was quite impressed with their tight harmonies. After coming off the stage, Cheryl and Sharon hugged me as soon as they could get to me, and then they introduced me to their dad. I learned they were hosts that night. The realization was slow in coming, but it dawned on me that these women were country music stars.

MEETING MINNIE PEARL

After I was in Nashville for a few years, some people convinced me that since I was so funny, I should at least try to make some money doing what came naturally. So, in my normal, academic way, I began to research the art form. I focused mainly on the character of Miss Minnie Pearl from Grinders Switch, created and portrayed by Mrs. Sarah Cannon. On April 22, 1990, I had the privilege of meeting Mrs. Cannon at an American Cancer Society fundraiser that she was co-hosting.

Again, my friend Tricia put me on the guest list since she was going to perform. Because I was with her, I was in the staging area not open to others, and that night I met Mrs. Cannon, a long-standing member of the Grand Ole Opry royalty.

Mrs. Cannon was gracious, classy, and obviously very intelligent. The only resemblance between her and her famous character with the price tag hanging from her hat was her trademark grin. I knew I had only a few minutes with her, so I got straight to the point: "Mrs. Cannon, when you are performing, do you go for the laugh or the heart of the audience first?" With absolutely no hesitation, she replied, "Oh, the heart! If you can get the audience's heart first, you will always get their laughter."

I then asked, "When you begin your comedy routine, do you follow the audience or make them follow you?" Just as quickly Mrs. Cannon said, "Oh, honey, you have to follow the audience or you will get nowhere. When I start my routine and sense the folks aren't going my way, I quickly try to find out where they are and follow them. If you don't, your routine will fall flat. Good luck with what you're doing."

The interview was kindly but definitely ended, as only a consummate performer used to dealing with the public can do. I did do the fan thing, asking her to autograph one of her cookbooks I had found in a used bookstore. I never even thought that she might wonder why I didn't bring a new one. The elegant Mrs. Cannon didn't bat an eyelash. She went for my heart first, and she got it.

LIKE A PIECE OF TRASH

When I was backstage that night, I was busy getting autographs on several programs as part of a fundraising effort. At one point I had exited through the door right off the stage into a large open area. Suddenly, a door at the other end of the room flew open, startling me. In came several muscular men, acting as if they were clearing the way through a crowd of imaginary fans for a very important person. In light of the fact that I was the only one back there, this behavior was odd. As I wondered who in the world would command such an entourage, Randy Travis walked through the door, followed by more big men.

I was thrilled! Adding the chart-topping Travis signature to my programs would greatly increase their value! As the group neared me, I stepped forward and said, "Excuse me, Mr. Travis. Would you mind signing my program?" By the reaction of the composite body-guard, you would have thought I was trying to throw myself at the star. The guard closest to me bodily moved me back, saying, "Mr. Travis can't sign that!" I looked back at Randy, and he had a look on his face that said, "I am so sorry. Wish I could help."

To say the least, I was stunned, and I silently watched as the bodyguards ushered Mr. Travis through the door to the stage. The man bringing up the rear turned toward me, walking backward through the door and looking as if he was ready to fend me off should I decide to attack the singer from behind. The door shut with a decisive bang, and I was standing there, blushing with shame and humiliation.

"God," I silently cried, "will I ever feel like I am worth anything? I was pushed aside like a piece of trash. You could have stopped Randy for one second to sign the stupid program. I don't really care who he is. I was just trying to collect his name for my charity. Please help me."

As silly as it sounds, the actions of a complete stranger spoke volumes to me about who I was.

HE THANKED ME

All of us have had events in our lives that we will remember for as long as we live. That particular night will be etched in my memory, not only because of what I just described, but also because of what happened next. God answered the silent prayer I had just prayed—and at the same time He answered the many impassioned requests of my little girl heart many years before.

As I stood there, I heard the now-familiar sound of the back door opening, the same door just used by Mr. Travis and his overzealous group of protectors. Wondering who else I would be endangering, I saw a man enter. Alone and unprotected, the King of the Cowboys—Roy Rogers himself!—walked through the door. Even as I write these words, I can feel another surge of adrenaline course through me just like the one I felt at that moment.

Wearing his signature white hat, a fancy Western suit, and gen-u-ine cowboy boots, Roy started walking my way, and I thought I was going to drop to the floor. My knees were weak; my mouth, dry. The blood pounded so loudly in my ears that it blocked out the music from the stage. I almost started to cry, but I guess somewhere I heard a little girl's voice say, "That's not the Cowboy Way."

As he drew closer, Roy smiled at me. He seemed to be expecting me to say something. My mind began to race: *Don't say anything stupid! Try to act like an adult woman instead of a little girl meeting Roy Rogers, her hero, after all these years!*

The mature words I was able to find in my shorting-out brain were, "May I have your autograph, Mr. Rogers? I've always been a big fan." As the nervous words tumbled out of my again cotton-dry mouth, I cringed with the realization that my hopes were dashed for impressing my hero with a brilliant line. However, Roy was as gracious as Mrs. Sarah Cannon had been. He took my programs (I had several) and signed each one with "Happy Trails! Roy Rogers and Trigger."

Handing back the signed programs, the King of the Cowboys thanked *me* before walking to the door that led to the stage and opening it himself. I found out later that he was there to both sing a duet with Randy and celebrate a colt, sired from Trigger's line, that Randy had purchased.

As the door closed behind him, I couldn't move. I looked around to see if anyone was in the area who could vouch for what had just happened. No one was around. I could hear the crowd yelling and applauding as Roy Rogers joined Randy Travis on the stage of the Grand Ole Opry, but time seemed to stop.

I felt like I was on laughing gas at the dentist as I remembered what I had read that very morning from Habakkuk 2:3 (NASB):

For the vision is yet for the appointed time; it hastens toward the goal, and it will not fail. *Though it tarries, wait for it; for it will certainly come, it will not delay.* (emphasis mine)

In retrospect, I'd had a fleeting thought earlier that day that something special might happen that night, but I had dismissed it without any hope. I learned early that having hope was a sure path to disappointment but not tonight.

THE KING OF THE COWBOYS AND THE KING OF KINGS

I was startled out of my reverie when the door to the stage opened again, and out came the front phalanx of Mr. Travis's troops. This time, however, I didn't care about the singer's autograph. After all, I had just met Roy Rogers. What happened next, though, was another inexplicable gift from God.

The same bodyguard once again put his arm out to guide the singing star past me, but Randy stopped walking. He put his hand up to the guard and walked the few steps to me. "Ma'am," he said, "I'm sorry I wasn't able to stop awhile ago, but I'll be glad to sign now."

You could have knocked me over with that proverbial feather. I handed Mr. Travis a program, and he signed his name. As he gave it back to me, he smiled and added, "Thank you very much. Have a nice night." He then looked at the less-than-happy muscle-bound guy as if to say, "*Now* we can leave."

I was rooted to that spot. How could so much have happened to me in those sixteen square feet! I was overwhelmed by how much Jesus clearly loved me. He knew the place that the King of the Cowboys had had in my child heart. The King of Kings had also known what I had needed in order to survive as a child, and through television and films He had given me Roy, a hero in whom I could place my trust. Now the Lord wanted me to trust Him and to know that He loves me—and again He gave me Roy, this time in person.

WITH APOLOGIES TO JIMINY

As I think back to that night, I find it hard to believe that, after more than thirty years, my dream came true. The King of the Cowboys had had my loyalty and the first place in my life when I was a child. Now, the King of Kings occupies that spot. Roy Rogers is still my hero, and occasionally I scan the auctions of his memorabilia on eBay, looking for my old lunch box that mysteriously disappeared from my bedroom while I was living in a house with three roommates who had many visitors.

That night outside the stage door of the Grand Ole Opry, I started believing again, and I later put these new words into the melody of my old friend Jiminy Cricket:

> If you trust in God's own Son
> Makes no difference what you've done.
> He has saved each tear you've cried
> 'Cause He loves you.

I'll let Roy Rogers, a man who also knew God's Son, close this story just the way he closed all his radio broadcasts, television programs, and personal appearances:

"Goodbye, good luck, and may the Good Lord take a likin' to you.

"Happy trails to you, 'til we meet again."[3]

The Stories I Keep

CHAPTER 4

LIFE LESSONS FROM A FRENCH GIRL AND A SPANISH GUY

In the summer of 1966, my dad was the pastor of a Baptist church in Gadsden, Alabama, a town about an hour northeast of Birmingham. My mother was a math and science teacher at Disque Junior High, and I was to be in the sixth grade in the fall. I don't know exactly when or why we were asked to have a foreign exchange student in our home for a month that summer, but Françoise (I am unsure of the spelling, but she pronounced it *Fran-swa-zee*) came to live with us.

I do not have a plethora of memories from our years at that church in North Gadsden, but the coming of this French girl who didn't shave her legs or underarms was interesting. I remember the first Sunday morning as we finished breakfast, Momma said, "Okay. We are running behind schedule, so we will have to get on the ball to be on time."

Our visitor flipped to a page in her French/American dictionary. With a puzzled expression on her face, Françoise asked my mom, "Where iz dis ball we are to get on?!" I can still hear my momma's infectious laughter. We all cracked up, and the normal atmosphere of being tense as strung wire about getting out the door to church on time was suspended for one day. Hallelujah!

SHOWING HER THE SOUTH

Although my parents didn't make much money, they tried to take Françoise to as many places as possible so she could experience real life in the American South. We went for a week to

Panama City Beach, Florida, where our visitor got a very deep tan except for the places her very limited bikini covered. I kept waiting for my dad or mom to tell her in no uncertain terms that she could not wear such a skimpy suit.

Not a word.

We also made several trips into Birmingham to eat at a nice restaurant (of which we had none in Gadsden at the time), see a movie, or shop.

Toward the end of her visit, I heard Françoise's voice raised in disagreement with my father (which is a whole other conversation), saying that she had not seen the real problems of segregation and racial violence because he had not taken her to the worst places. Although there had been terrible racial violence in Birmingham during the 1960s, I never witnessed any of it, nor do I remember seeing any television news reports of violence against blacks who simply wanted what was ordained by God: equal treatment. To this day I do not know if Françoise believed my dad's assurance that he had not kept her from anything.

Even though I don't remember any marches or sit-ins or boycotts, I do remember certain signs displayed in public places. Restroom doors, for instance, had "Colored" above the entrance, and placards in the windows or on the walls of businesses read, "We have the right to refuse service to anyone." Now, I can understand our visitor's doubts.

MY LOSS OF INNOCENCE

The first time I remember asking my momma about such a sign was at Pasquales, Gadsden's first pizza parlor. We didn't eat out often, but we went to Pasquales for birthday parties and to celebrate good report cards. My memory is sketchy, but my brain framed this particular moment and prominently hung it on the wall of my mind. Maybe we were waiting or maybe we were eating, but I saw the sign and asked Momma what it meant, because I couldn't image why a business would refuse a paying customer.

Momma's hesitation made me look at her. She was very careful in her wording: "RoseAnne, the sign means that the owner can refuse to serve someone just because he wants to."

I process information by putting pieces of information

in categories: my brain works much like a filing cabinet. That answer did not make sense to me. "But I don't understand, Momma. Why would the owner not serve food to someone who has money to pay?!"

My mom glanced at the lady behind the counter and then looked back at me. In a low voice, she replied, "Keep your voice down, sweetheart. It means they might not serve someone like Lillie Mae."

I was stunned. Lillie Mae had helped at our house in Ashville before we moved to Gadsden. She had taken care of my sister when Sherry was a baby while Momma taught junior-high English and chorus. Lillie Mae was at home when I came in from school, and she cared for me like I was her own.

It took a girl from France to tell me what was going on in my own backyard.

I wasn't hungry anymore.

PREJUDICE MEANS THE SAME THING IN SPANISH

A few years later, when I was in high school, Mom and Dad paid for me to spend a month in Spain. I was with other American students, but we lived in a dormitory on the University of Madrid campus, and we had teachers who were native to Spain. We were encouraged to venture into the city to explore as well as to practice our Spanish-speaking skills. Nightly events were planned for us American teenagers, but Spanish teens and even men in their twenties would somehow find their way into our parties.

Since I was one of the only ones who didn't drink alcohol, I was the designated lead-up-the-stairs-when-one-was-too-drunk-to-walk person. This assignment gave me the opportunity to observe the Spaniards when they thought everyone was too inebriated to notice or understand them. In those times, it was never hard to see their contempt for us, but I wasn't sure why they felt that way.

One day we met with some local teens who could speak English well enough for us to carry on an intelligent conversation. The first few hours of our visit were cordial and predictable: we talked about what America was like, what our hometown was like, what we did for fun. It was normal teenage banter. However, when we Americans were asked what we thought of Spain, one of us said he couldn't believe that more people didn't speak English, that there was almost nowhere to get "decent" food, and—the final blow—that the Spanish girls seemed stuck up to him, not friendly like American girls.

STRIKING A NERVE

With that, a young Spaniard from a small town outside of Madrid began to speak rapidly in his native tongue. I asked him to please translate what he had said and explain why he was upset. I've never forgotten his reply: "You Americans are arrogant pigs!" (No more Mr. Nice Guy!) "You come here with your better-than-you attitudes, rape our towns, dishonor our women, dismiss everyone who is not like you, and complain because we do not serve American food. You act as if we are backward and dumb, and you do nothing to hide your disdain. It is time for all Americans—you included—to get out of our country and never come back!"

I had done none of the things this Spanish teenager listed. As a matter of fact, I had been very careful to avoid such attitudes and statements. And I was the only one to respond to him: "Have I done any of the things for which you are angry? Have I shown you or anyone else from here any disrespect?"

When he didn't answer me, I continued, "It's true that this guy is what you are describing. But you can't lump all Americans into one group, just like we shouldn't make sweeping comments about all Spaniards!" I looked at him expectantly, hoping he would back down and maybe even apologize.

No such luck. This guy was steamed, and it didn't matter that he was treating me in the same way he claimed Americans treated his people. And I realized that our French foreign exchange student had done exactly what this young man had done: assumed that all Americans are arrogant and ignorant. The prejudice shoe was on another foot now—a Spanish one—and he was using it to stomp on me and on the rest of what he considered Yankee vermin.

Finally, we had to leave. Nothing had been resolved, no apologies were extended, and I will never forget that young man's face or his deep hatred of us just because we were Americans. Françoise's prejudice toward us was the same as this Spaniard's prejudicial judgment of us. I had been taught that we should love our neighbors as ourselves. Loving him back didn't seem like a gift he wanted.

LOOKING BACK

Now, years later, I hope that young Spaniard remembers me. Maybe he can now be honest with himself and recall at least one American who was different from what he thought and expected. I also hope Françoise is thinking favorably about me. I hope that I was—and am—different. After all, I have learned that in any culture, what goes around, comes around.

Adios.

Au revoir.

Amen.

The Stories I Keep

CHAPTER 5

HARPER LEE
AND ME

I taught ninth- and tenth-grade English at Homewood High School from 1979 until 1985 when I moved to Nashville. One of the required sophomore books was Harper Lee's classic *To Kill a Mockingbird*. It wasn't until my sophomore year in college that I had heard of the book. We moved in the middle of my junior year in high school, and in history I missed the whole Civil War. I imagine that's why I had not read this book.

SCOUT AND ME

I was in my second year at Samford University in Birmingham, and Dr. Atchison was my English professor. I can't say he was my favorite, but he gave me two important things I have never forgotten. First, in my freshman English class, he said, "You must learn the rules of grammar and composition. Once you know the rules, then—and only then—are you allowed to break them." I have used that permission almost every time I have written anything. The second important thing was his showing us the movie version of *To Kill a Mockingbird*.

As a girl raised mostly in small, Southern towns, I could relate to Scout Finch. Although she had more freedom of personal expression than I had as a child, we had in common the fact that our dad was a prominent person in the community, a man known by most people and respected by many. Also like Scout, my mom hired an African American woman, Lillie Mae, to help her with child care and housework.

Nothing like the Tom Robinson case happened in our little town, but Lillie Mae's house did burn to the ground, killing her baby grandson. As soon as my dad heard what had happened, he went to the black section of town, found Lillie Mae and the rest of her family, and did what he could to comfort them. His act was not viewed by everyone as either proper or appropriate, but public opinion cannot be one's moral compass.

Another thing for which Dad drew criticism was his inviting folks who lived in an area called Pinedale Shores as well as other "undesirables" to come to revivals and vacation Bible schools at our church. We had a 1962 Volkswagen Beetle with running boards. One of the most thrilling memories of my childhood was Dad's letting me stand on the running board on the driver's side while he held onto me tightly and drove slowly. When we reached a house, I would jump down and put a flyer on someone's door or in a mailbox and then jump back on for another s-l-o-o-o-w ride to the next place. Without me, of course, he also visited moonshiners up in the hills to invite their children to come to VBS.

As I read *To Kill a Mockingbird*—or *Mockingbird*, as Harper Lee calls it—I noticed many similarities between the world she described in Maycomb, Alabama, and my own. But, truthfully, it wasn't until Dr. Atchison showed the movie in class that I was forever connected to the characters of "Maycomb, a tired, old town." The scene that caused that bonding was when, in the empty courtroom, Atticus gathered up his papers at the defense table downstairs, but no one had left the upper balcony where the blacks had to sit. One by one every person upstairs stood in respect for the man who was putting his reputation and very life on the line to defend Tom Robinson, the black man accused of beating and raping a white girl, Mayella Ewell.

I was deeply moved as the folks in the balcony rose to their feet to honor Atticus, but I totally lost my composure when the Reverend Sikes said to Scout, "Stand up, Miss Jean Louise. Your father's passing." That is the most emotionally powerful visual I have ever witnessed on stage or screen. I am not sure I had even finished reading the book at that time, but that scene from the movie was pressed into my memory forever.

The Stories I Keep

HARPER AND ALICE

As I began to teach *TKAM* to my tenth-grade classes, many of the students were drawn into the story just as I had been in Dr. Atchison's class. For some, this was the first book they thought worth their while to read, and for some it actually was the first book of its length they had ever finished. One day some teachers coming back from lunchroom duty heard a group of kids talking in very animated tones. It turned out that they were discussing the *TKAM* characters and plot *outside* my classroom—and it wasn't even a homework assignment!

During these high-school teaching years, I began work on my master's degree in English at the University of Alabama in Birmingham. In the fall of 1980, I decided to try to contact Miss Harper Lee to ask her to speak to my students since they were so excited about her book.

As I thought about how to track down Miss Lee, I remembered something from *TKAM*. The young character Jem was angry with his father Atticus for not playing in a football game for the Methodists. Obviously, the Finch family attended the Methodist Church, so I deduced that Miss Lee might be a Methodist.

So my first call was to the Methodist Church, a number I found through directory assistance for Monroeville, Alabama, Miss Lee's hometown. No one answered the first time I called, but on my second try, I was able to speak to the secretary.

"Hi. I'm trying to get in touch with Miss Harper Lee. Would you be able to give me a number to reach her?"

"Why, sure I can. Let me just look that up for you."

The helpful secretary gave me the number, and I thanked her.

I wasn't sure what I would say when or if someone answered, but I really wanted her to encourage my students. So I took a deep breath and dialed the number.

The phone rang once … twice. In the middle of the third ring, someone answered in an authoritative voice that belonged to an older woman: "Hello?"

"Hi," I said. "May I speak to Miss Harper Lee?"

"She is unavailable at this time. I am her sister. May I help you?"

I remembered that her sister, Alice, was a lawyer who had retired from taking on cases and was helping the Methodist Church in Alabama.

"Yes, ma'am, I hope you can. I teach at Homewood High School in Birmingham. Well, actually it is a small community called Homewood in Birmingham." I began to sweat and wonder if I should have practiced my spiel before I was actually speaking to someone.

There was silence on the other end of the phone, so I launched in again.

"I have been teaching *To Kill a Mockingbird* to my sophomore classes, and my students are being changed by your sister's book. I was wondering if she would come speak to my classes—maybe to all the English classes—to inspire the students. Miss Lee could speak about anything she wanted. Of course, we would pay her way."

Now that I have been a public speaker for over twenty years, I laugh at how naïve I was, not realizing that Harper Lee's fee could be $10,000 or more. I thought I was being gracious to cover expenses.

Miss Alice Lee answered, "Oh, no. Harper couldn't come to your school. If she went to yours, she would have to go to every school that asked just to be fair. I'm sorry, ma'am, but Harper's coming is simply not possible."

As I thanked her and hung up the phone, I was very sad. I had been so excited about the possibility that my students would hear the woman who had written what was at one time the second best-selling book in the world, with the Bible being first.

I didn't put the Lees' phone number in a safe place, not even as a reminder of the fun I'd had getting the number. Why keep it? I didn't hold out any hope that I could get past Miss Alice and her understandable protection of her famous and reclusive sister.

IF AT FIRST YOU DON'T SUCCEED...

In the fall of 1982, I was nearing the end of my master's degree program. Since I was teaching *TKAM* for the fifth year straight, I had begun to recognize similarities between *TKAM* and Mark Twain's *Huckleberry Finn*. After some investigation, I realized that this parallel had not been the focus of much research at all. That fact was exciting in and of itself.

Although an introvert, I am fairly apt to jump off a ledge if there seems a remote possibility of success. With this burst of confidence, I decided to try to reach Harper Lee again. This time, however, I not only wanted to invite her to speak to my classes; I also wanted to ask her about my observation. I thought of myself as a news reporter asking a person to comment on a significant event. I would accept a door slamming in my face as well as, more likely, a polite refusal similar to the one I had already had from Miss Lee's sister.

So I again asked the directory assistance operator for the number of the Monroeville Methodist Church. When I rang that number, no one answered. An hour later I tried again, but still no answer. I didn't know how large Monroeville was, but I hoped it was still "small town" enough to support my knowledge of small-town relationships. In my experience, if the secretary of the Baptist Church—whom I was going to call next—was worth her salt, I was sure she would meet the challenge.

"Hello, ma'am. I'm trying to get in touch with Miss Harper Lee to ask her to speak to my students. The ladies at the Methodist church gave me the number some time ago, but unfortunately I lost it. Would you per chance know her number?"

"Hang on, honey," the voice said. She held the receiver away from her face and then said, "Hey, does anyone here know Nell Harper's phone number?"

When the secretary said both of Miss Lee's names as only a Southerner would, I knew immediately I had a real, live my-family's-been-here-long-enough-to-know-her-family resident of Monroeville, Alabama.

"Here you go, hon," the power broker said congenially.

Now I once again had to muster up the courage to dial the number, knowing that I would probably get Miss Lee's sister, Alice, once again. I don't remember praying for God's help, but at that time I don't think I had any hope that my prayers ever went further than the ceiling. My friend, Miss Helen Wright, once asked me if I believed God heard my prayers. I bowed my head, murmuring about not being good enough or something to the effect.

Her answer surprised this in-church-every-day-for-the-first-eighteen-years-of-my-life-except-for-conception preacher's daughter who was jaded from years of being a front-row observer of the backside of church people.

"Rose," Miss Helen Wright said, "since you don't believe God hears you, don't pray. I'll pray *for* you since I *know* He hears my prayers."

Later I found out that Jesus prays on my behalf constantly. In retrospect, since no one knew I was calling Harper Lee, there was no human being praying. Although the fact was hard for me to believe, Jesus must have mentioned the situation to His Father, because after three or four rings, a quiet voice with a gentle Southern accent said, "Heh-lo?"

I didn't remember Miss Alice's voice from the previous phone call, but I didn't have anything to lose. I said, "May I speak to Harper Lee?"

The voice replied, "This is Harper. Who is this?"

NOW WHAT DO I SAY?

Omigosh! Oh, man! I can't believe my ears! It worked! My plan worked! Harper Lee is on the other end of the phone! I was listening to the voice that so many had tried but failed to hear!

But the Pulitzer Prize winner was waiting for an answer. Have you ever wished you were someone else? How in the world could I answer her question with "This is RoseAnne Coleman, Miss Lee"?

I mean, who is that?

But I am not someone famous, so I had to be myself. I offered my name, quickly followed by "Miss Lee, you don't know me, but I called a few years ago and spoke with your sister to ask if you would come to Homewood High School in Birmingham to talk with my tenth-grade students. *Mockingbird* is the first book many of them get excited about, and I thought if maybe I could get you to come, it might change some of their lives."

I was talking fast, trying to get out my request before Miss Lee—understandably—hung up the phone.

"I know your sister Alice said you couldn't come, but I want to ask again if you could come to my school to speak."

I give credit to this world-famous, maybe multimillionaire, reclusive woman who was kind enough to engage in civil conversation with a total stranger without screaming at me for invading her privacy. After I paused for a breath, I heard Miss Lee chuckle. Even though I was as nervous as I had ever been because I was talking with a literary hero of mine, her laugh was inviting. Being the smart woman she is, maybe she knew I was tighter than the mainspring of an old windup clock and wanted to scrape me off the ceiling before she cussed me out.

Whatever the case, here is how the rest of our conversation went, as best as I can remember.

Chuckling, Miss Lee responded, "No, I couldn't come, but I appreciate the invitation. If I came to speak for your class, I would have to go to every place that asked."

I butted in. "Oh no, Miss Lee! We would keep your visit a secret. No one would have to know, so other places wouldn't be jealous."

Still chuckling, she said, "No, others would find out, so I cannot come to speak."

DETECTIVE WORK

After Miss Lee said that, I moved to a new level of panic: I realized she probably wanted to know how in the world I put my hands on her home number.

"Well, Miss Lee, I bet you are wondering how I obtained your private number."

Still in that quiet, refined voice, she asked, "How *did* you get it?"

"Okay. I knew the Finch family belonged to the Methodist Church, and I didn't think you would have the main characters be from another denomination than your own. So I called the Monroeville Methodist Church to ask for your number. However, the Methodists weren't home, so being a Baptist preacher's kid, I thought maybe the Baptist secretaries would know how to reach you. Evidently they did!"

"My goodness, RoseAnne, you are the detective!"

"Yes, ma'am, I guess I am. I have another question, Miss Lee, if you don't mind?"

"Go ahead. What is the question?"

"I'm working on my master's in English at UAB. I'm writing a paper on the similarities between Mark Twain's *Huckleberry Finn* and your *To Kill a Mockingbird*. Do you think you would be able to read it when I am finished?"

I have no idea why I made such a request of this world-famous author.

In a laughing voice, Harper Lee said, "Oh, no, I wouldn't be able to do that. In fact, I was typing a letter just now to someone at Harvard who asked if I would read his doctoral dissertation. If I helped him and you, I would have to help everyone else. I hope you understand."

In retrospect, I was grateful for her polite responses to me. I answered, "Yes, ma'am, I understand. I just don't understand why there is not more research on the similarities between *Huckleberry Finn* and *To Kill a Mockingbird*."

Then came the once-in-a-lifetime response, more evidence that Someone Whom God Hears must have been praying on my behalf. "Well, since you are such the detective, I am going to tell you something I have never told anyone else."

A SECRET SHARED

To be honest, my heart was about to fly out of my chest! I looked wildly around my bedroom, wondering if I had a recording device to get this never-before-revealed information on tape. Then I got upset that there was no one in the house to listen to what Miss Lee was about to say. I was the only one who heard what she said next.

Miss Lee continued. "I am going to tell you something I have never told anyone else: look at the similarities between *Tom Sawyer* and *Mockingbird*."

I was floored, "Wow, Miss Lee! I sure appreciate your telling me this. I will look at what I can find." I couldn't believe Harper Lee was telling me such a secret!

Then the clock must have struck midnight because Miss Lee asked, "Where are you calling from?"

"I'm in Birmingham," said the pumpkin, aka RoseAnne.

"Oh my! This call must be costing you lots of pennies!"

"Please don't worry about that, Miss Lee! I consider these pennies well spent," I sputtered.

"I didn't know you were calling from Birmingham!" she replied.

"Yes, ma'am. This is where I teach."

"Well, I need to let you go so you don't spend all your money. It's been nice talking to you," the reclusive woman said. "You have a nice night."

"Thank you, Miss Lee. I appreciate your speaking with me, especially telling me to look at *Tom Sawyer*."

"Yes, well, you look at *Tom Sawyer* and *Mockingbird*."

"Thank you, Miss Lee. Good night," I wistfully replied.

"Good night to you," she said.

As I hung up the phone, I slid down the wall by the chaise upon which I had been sitting while we spoke. It was hard to believe:

1. Not only had I found Miss Lee's phone number, but she had answered when I called.
2. Not only had she answered, but she had talked with me for about ten minutes.
3. Not only had she talked with me, but Harper Lee had told me something about *To Kill a Mockingbird* that she admittedly had never told anyone else. It was a special present for me!

I never spoke another sentence to this woman I had been dreaming of calling for several years, a woman who was kind enough to take the call of a stranger who had been given her private number by the secretary at the Baptist church.

ENOUGH

In the Pulitzer Prize-winning *To Kill a Mockingbird*, Mr. Arthur "Boo" Radley was an elusive, secretive man throughout the narrative. Because everyone in the small town had conflicting stories about him, the children's fantasies about Boo were fueled by what others had said, tales that stoked the fire of their own imaginations.

However, at book's end, Boo asked Scout to take him home. She led him by the hand through her house like a child, but on the porch made Boo crook his arm for her to take it as a lady would. Then they walked slowly, as if she were being escorted by a gentleman, in case Mrs. Stephanie Crawford was watching from her upstairs window.

After Mr. Arthur went inside his house, Scout stood just for a few minutes on the Radley front porch to see what her world looked like from there. Her point of view forever changed. Her conclusion is one of the classic lines in literature: "Atticus was right. One time he said you never really know a man until you stand in his shoes and walk around in them. Just standing on the Radley porch was enough."[1]

After my delightful conversation with Miss Lee—a conversation no doubt arranged by the God of the Methodists *and* the Baptists—I felt much like Scout: I hadn't needed to stand and walk around in Miss Harper Lee's shoes. Just talking to her on the phone was enough.

CHAPTER 6

(MOTHER'S) EXPERIENCE WAS THE BEST TEACHER

When I started teaching at age twenty-two, Momma had been in the profession for twenty-one years. She helped me see that being a teacher requires knowing how to be both a politician and a ringmaster of a circus that has at least three rings, as well as being an educator. One bit of her hard-earned wisdom has proven true no matter what hierarchy I find myself in: get on the good side of the support personnel, because if they don't like you, they will make your life hellacious. Since Momma used profanity rarely, her word choice had the impact she intended. "Start with the head secretary and work your way down" were her next words to me as I packed my lunch in the new leather briefcase she had bought me, reminiscent of the red plaid book bag she had given me as I walked out the door to start first grade.

MY FIRST DAY

On my first day as a junior-high English teacher, I arrived at the school early and went to the main office. The head secretary was already there. I was only twenty-two, and she thought I was a student. Since I didn't look much older than some of the seniors, she wouldn't be the only one to make that mistake that day.

"Can I *help* you?" the sixty-something lady said, obviously irritated and looking back down at what she had been doing when I came in. Even though I knew I was being dismissed, I jumped in.

"Yes, ma'am," I replied. "I'm RoseAnne Coleman, the new seventh-grade English teacher."

When I heard a muffled "Good," I realized that the information didn't seem to warrant her standing up in welcome. I continued speaking to the part of her head that was visible at counter level.

"My mom is a teacher, and she said the first thing I needed to do was to meet you, because you can make my life easy or hard." I probably should have rephrased my momma's statement into something less forward, but it was too late.

Standing to her full height of 5 feet and 2 inches, the woman sized me up like the kind of experienced horse trainer who has no sense of humor but produces Kentucky Derby winners.

"That's what she said, did she?" Her response sounded more like a challenge than a question.

"Yes, ma'am. She sure did."

"Just where did your mother get her education?" quizzed the head secretary.

"What is now the University of Montevallo," I answered.

The woman seemed to weigh that information for a moment and then pronounced, "Well, that school puts out good teachers."

Leaning toward me, she said, "Well, Miss Coleman, I have a lot of work to do before the place is overrun with students." Dismissing me with no apology, she turned and went into the principal's office.

VICTORY!

During class changes, the teachers were required to stand at their doors to police the traffic in the halls and, at assigned times, check the restrooms closest to their classroom. Mine was right next door to the junior-high girls' restroom, and up until that point of the day, taking the short walk between classroom and restroom to check the facilities was the easiest thing I had done.

On my first reconnaissance, I wondered what in the world I was supposed to check while I was in the restroom without looking like a voyeur. The first thing I saw, however, was an older girl holding a lighted cigarette at the far end of the room. She was standing halfway in the stall. When she saw me, she turned slightly toward the toilet as if she might ditch the evidence. A few seconds passed, and then she nonchalantly took another puff.

I walked over to her and said, "You were right the first time: I *am* a teacher."

Taking the smoking gun from her hand, I then took her arm and escorted her to the main office. When we entered, Mrs. Cain looked at me, at the girl, and at the lighted cigarette. I simply stated, "I just caught this young lady smoking in the junior-high girls' restroom."

The comment of that school's power broker will forever ring in my ears: "Good job, Miss Coleman! We've been trying to catch her for a year, and you did it on your first day! When you told me your momma was from Montevallo, I *knew* you would be a good one! You go on back to class, and I'll take it from here."

Although I was shaking inside after my first act of disciplining a student, I thanked God for my momma as I walked back to my classroom door—and that was not the last time she threw me a rope in my quicksand!

I have found experience is the best teacher, even if it's not your own.

The Stories I Keep

CHAPTER 7

A WOMAN WHO LAUGHED AT THE FUTURE

Success is not final, failure is not fatal: it is the courage to continue that counts. — Winston Churchill

One has had to live through difficult times to know the truth of Churchill's words. Some think having money is the answer to life; some think it's fame. However, when a person is staring death squarely in the face, no money or fame or success is worth a thin dime. Courage is the only currency that purchases anything when death demands payment. But I'm getting ahead of myself.

Allow me to introduce my mother, Mary Melrose Bibles Coleman. In the 1950s my mother majored in home economics and minored in science, but she reversed these subjects in real life: science was the major teaching focus of this brilliant woman's life. As for applying what she learned in home economics, she jokingly said that the most useful tool she learned to use was a can opener. Having a full-time job outside the home as a schoolteacher, Momma didn't get home until 4:00 or 4:30 after a full day of work. With Dad's liking supper on the table at 5:00, I grew up thinking that home cooking meant food that was heated at home.

In order to appease and please the hungry, Mom did the best she could with what she had. That meant meals were quick and easy. With a job, a family, and church responsibilities, she just didn't have much time left for food preparation. Although her maternal grandfather and her own mother had raised fruits and vegetables to serve in season and then can for the winter, Momma married a preacher who had no interest in planting vegetable seeds in the Alabama dirt; he was too busy planting seeds in people's heart for another kind of harvest.

Once, when someone asked me to name my favorite dish prepared by my mother, I replied, "Toasted saltine crackers." I didn't think anything about it, but years later I heard Momma laughingly repeat my answer to a friend, saying she had "just about died" when I said that. I defended her by saying that no one else's mom toasted crackers! I thought I was defending Momma's honor, but she and her friend just laughed even more.

With this upbringing, I am not in the health food store very often. Furthermore, since I was familiar with the smell of cotton poison in our rural area of Alabama, I didn't hear the word organic until I was in my thirties. And until someone suggested I buy food from the farmers and ranchers in my area—and my friend Shirley began teaching me to cook—I could not taste the difference between the $4-a-pound organic green beans and Kroger's $1.99 ones.

Yet, I was well aware of a local bakery's delicious sunflower seed bread, but I enjoyed it only on special occasions because I would have to drive over an hour for a loaf. I was thrilled when someone told me that a local health food store was carrying it. As I was checking out, I found something even more satisfying than that bread. On a magnet lying in the space between the conveyer belt and the check-writing stand, I read this Albert Einstein quote: "Out of clutter, find simplicity. From discord, find harmony. In the middle of difficulty lies opportunity." This quote reminded me of my mother.

A WOMAN OF COURAGE

Melrose Bibles Coleman was the kind of woman described in Proverbs 31:25— "Strength and dignity are her clothing, and she laughs at the time to come" (ESV). This truth, combined with Einstein's observation, provides a snapshot of Mom: she was, metaphorically speaking, a smart dresser who found simplicity, harmony, and opportunity in every aspect of her life—as a public school teacher, as a pastor's wife, and as a mom.

Since my dad was attending college on the GI bill, Momma had to be the breadwinner for our family, and I was placed in a nursery school in 1955, a situation that was not at all the norm for a 1950s family. Yet my mother's parents had done without many things so that their daughter could get her college education. I remember my maternal grandmother saying that she wanted Melrose to escape the life of working as hard as she had had to do, "ruining" her hands and pushing her body to its physical limits just to get by.

No matter how much we try to shield the next generation from the pain we ourselves have endured, each life has its own share; the only difference is the packaging. So, ironically, Momma had to work just as hard as her mother had, but the lines on my mother's face were from laughter, not from stoically facing life as something to be endured, which was my grandmother's approach. But, in sharp contrast to how she had been treated by her mother, Marie Bibles did let Melrose know that she was loved very much, and Nannie supported my mom in every endeavor. No wonder courage characterized Mom's life. She had a good teacher.

In addition to being courageous, Mother was the most intelligent person and one of the most brilliant communicators I have ever met. She was able to juggle an amazing number of metaphorical balls at work without drawing attention to herself. When she retired, it took five folks to replace her.

Although my mom was known for many things in life, it was her laughter that people most remember. I have often said that if I were in a room with a hundred people, I would know that my mother was present if I heard her laugh. I learned from Mom to laugh easily, but I am still trying to master smiling at the future. I am also still seeking to have the kind of burning hope Momma seemed to have despite all the difficulty she faced in life. It is true that my mother taught me much about how to live in this world, but when she battled cancer for a second time, she also taught me how to die to this world and prepare for the next.

THE FINAL PHASE OF THE JOURNEY

What follows are excerpts from the journal I kept during the last days of Melrose's life—and this is one story I wish I *weren't* keeping, but one that I will never let go of it.

I am a changed woman because of this experience. Emotionally, I crashed and burned almost a year after Momma's coma and death, and I am still dealing with the pain of losing her.

Yet, as I reread the journal entries, I am amazed at the many ways God made His presence very clear to me even though I *felt* so very much alone.

Wednesday, December 16, 1998

Sacred Heart Hospital, Pensacola, Florida
Momma was sleeping when I arrived at the hospital after driving from Nashville.

Thursday, December 17, 1998

Mom was still in what seemed to be a very deep sleep. A nurse administered what was described as a very expensive hormone shot to stimulate her adrenal gland. Before the nurse had even finished giving the shot, Momma opened her eyes. Her whole face lit up when she saw me between the bedrails. She waved, saying in a very sweet, childlike voice, "Hey, RoseAnne!" I was shocked. I answered, "Hey, Momma! Welcome back!" She was awake much of the rest of the day. What a gift! How I wish I had told her in the past how much her love means to me.

Friday, December 18, 1998

Momma began to experience severe headaches, which were attributed to her blood pressure rising.

Sunday, December 20, 1998

Today is Mom and Dad's forty-fifth wedding anniversary. Dad brought in forty-five roses in two vases and three in another to say, "I love you." He also bought her diamond earrings, but Momma didn't respond except to look at her presents. Sherry put the earrings on her, and I put the red hat I had bought her at Eddie Bauer. We arranged the flowers around her chair, and Dad took her picture.

At the time none of us realized it would be the last photograph we would ever take of Momma. She had a determined, thin-lipped smile, and we later noticed her left hand was curled up and clinched—a sign of the building pressure in her brain.

Monday, December 21, 1998

Mom didn't want anything to eat. Her head was really hurting her. We put her in the chair, thinking that the change of position would help ease the pain. Dad wanted breakfast, and I asked Sherry to accompany him. He seemed very unsettled, and she is able to communicate with him better than I am.

Right after they left, Momma wanted to go the bathroom. As she was washing her hands, she took the paper towel and wiped down the sink just as she did at home. She stood there just pushing the paper towel back and forth for some time. When she had been back in the chair a little while, I noticed Momma's left leg began to shake. I asked if she was cold and wanted to be back in bed. When she nodded her head, I helped her stand as we normally did: she put her arms around my neck as I hugged her under her arms.

This time when Momma put her arms around my neck, though, she rested her head on my shoulder. It was a special moment. All of a sudden, she went limp and collapsed in my arms. I panicked because I didn't have a good hold on her, and we were too far from both the bed and the chair to quickly get her to either one.

I sort of heaved her into the chair—it was a little closer than the bed—and saw that her eyes were fixed as if she were looking upward to her right without turning her head. The word *SEIZURE* exploded in my brain. I ran to the door and yelled for help. When no one came, I ran back and screamed, "My mom's having a seizure!" The nurses rushed in and started talking to Mom, trying to get her to respond. She was not breathing.

The doctor ordered an anti-seizure IV that helped.

About an hour later, I was standing at the end of the bed, and I realized Mom wasn't breathing. I yelled to Sherry and to the nurses' station. This time five or six ran in like a flood with a crash cart. I stood to the side, telling Momma to breathe, to hang on, to stay with us.

The oncologist was called; he asked to speak to a family member. Sherry went. Then she called my name. "Dr. Patton wants to know if we want to resuscitate her or not!" I looked at her incredulously. "Of course we do!"

As the nurses pushed Mom's bed into the hallway, they

instructed me to keep telling her to breathe. I felt like I was living out a scene from a movie. Five of us were running, pushing and pulling the bed down the hallway, to CCU. The nurses were talking to one another while I kept yelling at Mom to stay with me, to breathe, to not die.

After we got her into CCU, I was told to wait outside. Walking back out those metal doors was one of the hardest things I have ever done. As I stood alone in the hallway, I was crying and scared, not knowing if Mom was alive or dead.

Momma's seizures had been caused by pressure resulting from cancer cells in the spinal fluid. Although the MRI had shown no growth of cancer in the brain, the cancer was attacking and destroying the brain's surface.

When the doctor said that, I remembered the last time I had been home, the last time I saw Mom fully herself. She had been standing in front of the icemaker. As she closed the door, Momma leaned on the handle and said, "As a scientist, I know too much. I know that when there is cancer in the lung, it usually goes to the brain." She was right.

Dr. Patton said we could take her off the respirator and let Momma go. Dad asked if there were any treatment at all that could be done. The doctor said there was one, but it had poor results at best—and it came with terrible side effects. Dad said we needed to at least give Momma a chance. Then Dr. Patton asked an excruciating question: Were we sure we wanted to "bring her back around, wake her to realize she had new cancer outbreaks, just to decline all over again"?

How could there be any good answer to that question other than a loud NO? But that wasn't the answer we were prepared to give.

Wednesday, December 23, 1998
When I began this journal on Thanksgiving Day last year, November 27, 1997, who would have guessed that this entry would be written as I sat by the bed of my beloved momma? Who would have guessed she would be lying in a coma. Oh, that this were fiction or someone else's story.

I just wrote a friend:

As I sit here watching my sedated mom, listening to Windham Hill Winter Solstice V, I am comforted by the familiarity of the music. I am stricken with the realization that this vigil is a slippery slope down to death—my own beloved mother's mortality resting lightly between this world and the mansion prepared for her by our Savior. She had to be sedated, even while in a coma, because her agitation has steadily increased. I have so many questions: *Does she hear me? Does she know me? Will we ever speak in this life again? Will God really heal her? Will she ever look at me again?* I still have hope, praying she gets off the ventilator. However, her shallow breathing indicates that she is too weak. Oh, the agony of this time!

Yet, underneath all the pain, running like an underground stream, course the words of Psalm 116, the psalm God gave me one year ago today. As I stand at the edge of this day, I take a backward glance and see that God's faithful preparation for this time is quite evident. Although my heart is crushed, I am humbly grateful for the love and care of my Savior and Beloved Husband.

Thursday, December 24, 1998, 4:15 a.m.

At the moment, Mom is resting and still. This usually lasts only a few moments, then she's moving and wiggling in discomfort. I came in here about 2:30, having slept since about midnight, I guess. Dad is sleeping more than Mom, Sherry, or me. I brought my old guitar from home. Sherry and I sang Christmas carols to Momma. All the nurses came in the room to listen, and several wiped tears from their eyes. I realized that in order to take care of Momma, these folks were away from their own families. I have a new appreciation for health-care workers.

I am also seeing that God has a purpose for everything that happens. If Momma hadn't been in a coma, we wouldn't have been at the hospital to bring Christmas into the CCU for the nurses and the other patients who could hear our singing.

Christmas Day, Friday, December 25, 1998, 4:03 a.m.

Mother lies in a coma. Dad and Sherry sleep in a waiting room. I keep a holy vigil, watching Your little lamb by night … Come into my darkness, O Light of Heaven … Fill my heart with the hope of joy in this world because the Lord has come. Shine Your light into Momma's body, into her mind. Heal her, Lord God Almighty. I believe, Lord, but help my unbelief. I cannot be stoic like Sherry, but maybe we are the same: struggling to stay afloat in an ocean of fear. God, You gave us Your Son in a simple moment, and I would ask that in this simple moment You would do a simple miracle for Momma.

2:30 p.m.

You know, Lord, It would seem to be from Your divine Hand that a wandering mother dog would find shelter in my carport on Christmas Eve and that you provided my neighbor to care for her and the babies. Thank You for showing me that You care for mothers and children, guiding them into havens that You have prepared. …

I dressed up for Christmas Day because I knew Momma would want us to acknowledge Your birth, but neither Dad nor Sherry said anything. I know our minds are scattered, but this family thing is hard.

Thursday, December 31, 1998, 12:53 a.m.

This has been a rough twenty-four hours. Momma was agitated through the night; she didn't get easy until 4:45. Dr. Patton came in about 6:15 a.m., and his report was grim: Mom's cancer count had gone from 30 to 170-ish *with* the treatments, and he thinks we need to stop. But Dad said if she were to die right now, he'd be a mess. It seems we are never prepared for death. Unfortunately this is true for my dad—and for me.

A sweet moment happened this afternoon when I told Momma that I love her. She surprised me by immediately responding with "I love you too." Thank You, Father, for such a gift! Hearing Momma respond to me—I know You didn't have to allow that, but I am grateful that You did.

Father, are You going to take my beloved mother home to You? Once again You give me hope through Your Word:

This God is our God forever and ever:
he will be our guide even unto death.
— Psalm 48:14

Hitherto hath the LORD helped us. — 1 Samuel 7:12b

Friday, January 1, 1999, 1:30 a.m.
St. Catherine's, Sacred Heart Hospital

They moved us here this morning. Sherry woke me right before Mom was wheeled out. I had to lie down at 5:30 because I couldn't stand up any longer.

Sherry and I both have definite beliefs about Momma's healing: I believe God can heal her; Sherry believes God *will*. I admired my little sister's tenacious belief. I, however, had seen God answer prayers for other sick people in my world by granting them eternal healing, so I knew God's answer might be different from what we desperately wanted for our mother.

Dad told me with great surprise and grief that it seems we will have to move Momma to a "health-care facility." I told that to Sherry, and his statement bothered her greatly because she thought it didn't show faith that Momma would be healed. "Momma will go nowhere but home," she declared.

Lord, I do not know what You have in store for any of us. I told Sherry that You would provide for the path that You have chosen for us. And that is a good reminder in this new year, Lord, for You have always been faithful.

I guess each family deals with a crisis differently. Our history has not been one of calm responses, and Momma has always been the one keeping our boat from sinking completely. With her in a coma, the stress level is through the roof. My world has shifted off its foundation, teetering on the edge of an abyss, smoking from the wildfires of fear, anger, and despair.

Saturday, January 2, 1999, 3:30 a.m.

I took over at 1:45 a.m. Mom had what seemed to be another set of seizures. She is now sedated but still periodically restless. We were all pretty scared. By the end of the event, we were at each other's throats.

As a whole, we do not do well together without her. It is so hard to remember You are in control.

4:05 a.m.
Please get me through another night's watch here, Lord. How do I pray for my sweet momma? For some reason—maybe due to my lack of faith—it doesn't seem that You are healing Mom to remain in this world.

To see Mother in such a helpless state, suffering so, is one of the most difficult things You have asked me to do. Are You going to come for her? You are shaking me up, Lord, in all areas of my life. Please show me how to walk in Your presence, Lord. Help me to be strong and courageous, and not be dismayed.

4:30 a.m.
Yes, Mom will die, but how or when is still in Your hands, Lord.

> *Set your affection on the things above, not on things on the earth.* — Colossians 3:2

> *"O death, where is thy sting? O grave, where is thy victory?"* — 1 Corinthians 15:55

5:31 a.m.
I read today "You will never learn faith in comfortable surroundings."

Wednesday, January 13, 1999, 10:05 a.m.
Nashville, Tennessee
It is good to be home, but even home is different when I realize my momma will probably never come to visit again, that she is dying. How horrific is that series of words: She is *dying*. I am coming to see that a part of me is dying, too.

Sunday, January 17, 2008
Pensacola, Florida
Mom was in obvious pain, bloated from the liquid in the feeding tube and in respiratory distress from the fluid buildup. Sherry called

me, and I arrived here about 11:30 last night.

The day was calm until the evening when the nurse came into the room and said we had to make a decision about Momma's feeding tube. Confused, I asked her to explain. What she said made a cold chill sweep my whole being.

Momma's feeding had been disconnected earlier on "family's orders." I knew the nurse had wrong information and needed to restart the feeding immediately. Mom had been without fluid for almost twenty-four hours!

When Sherry returned, I told her about the mistaken withholding of food. She stormed to the nurse's station. Five minutes later Dad arrived, wanted to know what was going on, and then he went up there. Momma and I just stayed in the room. (As I write that, I think I can hear Momma's laughing.)

This is so hard. In her living will Momma had stated not to withhold food or water if she were unconscious and couldn't request sustenance. However, compliance with her wishes is causing her lungs to begin to fill with fluid and mucus. All within me says she is going to die—barring, of course, the miracle of her being healed of the cancer, her brain's being restored, and her being raised up from this coma.

How can we make such a choice: to continue feeding in faith that she will recover or to discontinue feeding, a decision that will certainly lead to her death? Are we hearing Your voice on Mom's behalf?

Dad has been a pastor for over forty years, I make my living teaching the Bible to women, Sherry is on the praise team music group at her church—yet we seem to have heard different things from You about what's going to happen. Since I think You are going to heal her by bringing her Home to You and they believe You are going to raise her for more time in this world, I am grieved that there seems to be no talking aloud about what may happen, how we are feeling, how we are relating to one another in this unimaginable situation.

Anger, fear, exhaustion, desperate hope and hopelessness, uncertainty—these are our companions in this room, along with sweet Melrose who does not have to referee anymore. I wonder if she can still hear us.

Monday, January 18, 1999
What an awful time I've had in this day! Mom's sodium level was 107 (I think normal is in the 140-ish range). About an hour later, I remembered that when Mom's sodium level dropped to 117 in the hospital, they gave her a 5-percent solution very quickly. I went to the nurse's station. When I said, "107," the head nurse exclaimed, "107! That's critical!"

She went to look for Momma's nurse, who came back with a sandwich in her hand, obviously angry that I had raised the issue. She said she would call the pharmacy again. I said aloud to all: "Sacred Heart is not that far away. I'll go get the bag!" No one answered me.

Wanting to hear the call, I followed the angry nurse into an empty room. While she was on hold, she said cattily, "I *thought* I had explained all this to you, but *obviously* I did not make it clear"—to which I replied, "Yes, I understood, but my mother needs that bag here more quickly because 107 is critical." She butted in, "I *know* it's critical. I'm a nurse!" (Later Sherry said the same nurse told her that she knew what she was doing because she had made a C average in nursing school. *Great.*)

The nurse's attitude and responses stunned me. I had to keep myself from grabbing her and saying, "My mother is *dying*, and you're talking to me this way?!" I have had to calm myself so many times through this ordeal that my insides are sore and my brain feels like it is going to explode.

As I listened to the one-sided call, I realized they had not even sent the bag yet.

Angry, I went back to Momma's room. About five minutes later, our friends Carolyn and Bo came to visit. Both work at the hospital, but I had forgotten that Bo is in charge of the lab. When I told him the sodium level, he had a fit. "I have never even seen one that low at the hospital! Melrose could die any minute!" He confronted the nurse, but Momma still had no sodium bag.

At about 2:00 the nurse came into the room to call the hospital again. She was told that the bag had been sent. Finally, at

2:30, a cab driver walked into Momma's room with the sodium bag in his hand. When I asked him what had taken so long, he seemed confused because he had only been called at 2:15. I shook his hand and thanked him, saying that he probably had saved my mother's life. …

When the nurse left the room, I sat down by Momma's bed. Looking at her motionless body, I said, "Momma, I'm sorry it took me so long to get that sodium bag. I'm doing my best to care for you, but this is one hellacious situation."

My heart and head felt as if they were going to burst with the pressure, with the stress, with the grief.

Wednesday, January 20, 1999, 11:35 a.m.
Since Momma's breathing is beginning to sound labored, we are turning her every ten minutes, trying to induce a coughing reflex. However, she is like a rag doll, absolutely limp, and no cough is coming. Pat said that inertia sometimes is a sign of disease progression. Sherry didn't want to hear what she said. Be with my baby sister, Lord.

1:15 p.m.
A breathing treatment, a feeding, a suctioning, the arrival of my father … Now I can sit down to read, and I feel that You have prepared every day's devotional reading just for me and just for this time. I have to admit that sometimes I wonder if You are real, but in this moment, I am stunned into silence that I serve the Living God.

> Every person and every nation must take lessons in God's school of adversity. We can say, "Blessed be the night, for it reveals to us the stars." In the same way we can say, "Blessed is sorrow, for it reveals God's comfort."[1]

Lord, please show me Your sovereign truth in these statements. In my flesh I do not want Your lessons; I want my mother well.

Friday, January 22, 1999, 8:30 a.m.
I think that these folks will be very glad when the family in Room

511-A goes home. Two doctorates and one master's degree all taking care of one comatose woman have not presented a normal family dynamic. I find that even in my deep sorrow, I can hear Momma's laughing with me about this. I wonder if she can still hear us. I tell her constantly that I love her, that I am proud of her, that she is free to go, although selfishly I want her to stay.

I hadn't been here long when Momma opened her eyes! For a second I thought the movement might just be a reflex of some sort, but when our eyes locked, she closed her eyes and the corner of her mouth lifted in a weak but definite smile. The Bible is true when it says you can see one's soul through the eyes.

My beloved mother opened her eyes again and, to my surprise, tried to say something to me. When I didn't understand her, I asked, "Ma'am?" This is a Southern child's way of asking, "What did you say?" Momma widened her eyes, lifted her eyebrows, and pulled her head back a little bit as if to say, "I appreciate your being so respectful." I replied, "Well, Momma, you've always taught me to be courteous."

Momma closed her eyes as she smiled. It was hard to see her so very weak, but I was overcome by the gift of her coming back to us.

As she rested, we waited, stationed all around her bed: Sherry to her left, Dad at the foot of the bed, and I to her right. When her eyes opened again, Momma gazed at Sherry for a little while and then closed her eyes.

I couldn't read her expression when Mom looked at Dad, but when she finally looked at me, her intent was clear. Mustering her last bit of strength and looking straight into my eyes, Momma communicated her love for me. Although she was known for her amazing verbal skills, Momma didn't need words. Her eyes said it all.

Although I didn't know it then, that was the last time I would look into my mom's beautiful blue eyes and see her looking back. Soon she slipped back into the coma. I fell asleep in a recliner in the room until I suddenly awoke abruptly at 5:45 a.m. Sherry and Dad were on either side of Momma's bed, suctioning her throat. They were trying to clear the mucus that was making her breathing so laborious. Mom was gasping, her chest heaving with the effort.

I told them to take a rest because I was awake now. As they both turned away from Momma, I immediately saw that Momma couldn't breathe. She was trying, but the fluid had finally filled her lungs, and she was drowning. I have never felt so helpless in my life. I got behind her, trying to hold her straight, hoping she could draw a little air. She couldn't.

Momma was suffocating, and her attempts to breathe began to lessen. All of a sudden I realized that we must be in the presence of the Lord and the angels, coming to get this faithful servant, to take her to heaven. I tried to sing one of her favorite choruses. "Jesus, Jesus, Jesus/There's something about that Name" was all I could croak out of my cotton-dry mouth. I then yelled that we needed to pray, but Sherry and Dad were trying to cope in their own way that Mom was actually dying despite their best efforts and most fervent prayers.

I was holding Momma when she stopped breathing. As I stood by the bedside, I comprehended for the first time in my life the price of Adam and Eve's disobeying God. The chasm that now separated my beloved mother and me was not what God had intended. We were created for fellowship with God and with one another, but a little before 6:00 a.m. on Saturday, January 23, 1999, death tore Mother from my grasp.

This moment marked the end of thirty-eight days of caring for Mom. Around the clock we had fervently been guarding the flickering flame of a precious heart, but in the end the winds of death were just too strong. Although I had thought that God was preparing me for Momma's death, now that she was gone, I was overcome with a grief that slashed at my mind and my soul, taking away my strength.

We just sat around the bed, stunned, I guess, and maybe hoping that God would still perform a miracle, that Mom would awaken like Jairus's daughter did in Luke 8:40-56, and that our mourning would turn to unspeakable joy. However, as I sat there, my hopes were dashed when I heard the death rattle, the closing of the door between this world and the next.

A LESSON FROM THE BATTLE

Several years after Momma's death, I was on my knees planting pansies in my front yard. Suddenly my brain registered Momma's speaking to me: "Hey, darlin'. Those pansies are gorgeous."

Honestly, I didn't know what to think. I said, "Momma? Is that you?! Jesus, is that Momma?!" I didn't get a response from Him, but it was as if Mom and I conversed a little bit about the pansies. We both loved digging in the dirt and watching things grow.

The last time Mom and I were together at home, I had asked her what she had learned from her battle with cancer. After a few minutes of silence, she had replied, "To always be ready." I knew she meant ready to die, ready to meet Jesus.

So, on this day in the yard, I thought I would ask a follow-up question. "Well, Momma, now that you are in heaven, what would you say you have learned?" The answer that came staggered me.

"RoseAnne, I have learned that God is more trustworthy than we could have ever imagined. You can trust Him."

I didn't hear anything else, and I sat down at the edge of the pansy bed. "God, I do not know whether or not I just had a conversation with my mother; but I do know that what I heard could not have come from the evil one. In the voice of the one I trust more than anyone else, I heard that I can trust You. Please help me to do just that. Please help me trust You."

Maybe the whole thing was the result of a heatstroke; maybe I had a momentary mental breakdown; maybe the evil one was playing a terrible trick on me; or maybe I really heard Momma say that God is more faithful than we could have ever imagined—and that I can trust Him.

As I sat back on my heels pondering Mom's—God's—message from beyond the pale, I tried to reconcile the Lord's unfailing faithfulness with Mom's two battles with cancer, the last battle leading to what I considered her untimely death. My mind was scuttling back and forth between belief and doubt like a sand crab on the shore. How could my thimble-sized intelligence possibly work through such a God-sized conundrum!

Suddenly, a scene flashed across my mind's eye. It was much

like what I imagined happening when the evil one stood before God's throne in the first chapter of Job. It was as if I could hear Satan demanding that he be granted permission to give Momma cancer again. Laughing, God said, "That is an excellent idea. But first I'm going to give Melrose eighteen years to develop a sphere of encouragement that will include oncologists, nurses, technicians, cancer patients and their families, orderlies, secretaries, and many others. Also, I'm going to change her elder daughter's life because of her mother's courageous journey home. RoseAnne will learn amazing lessons from the suffering and grief."

DEFINITELY WORTH KEEPING

Why is such a traumatic story one I will keep and I share?

A person's story can change a life, and I want each person who reads this to know how important it is to be changed by the Truth and then, in turn, to share the story so others might be changed. Isn't that the Gospel?

I also hope that, by my telling this story, you are encouraged to believe that God knows your name, that He is with you every moment, and that He is more trustworthy than you can imagine. In this chapter alone, you have walked with me through some of the most costly but significant acreage of my life.

As I look at the land of my life, some of the fields are cleared; some are still overgrown with weeds. Some fields are newly planted and needing rain from heaven to stay alive. Some are producing fruit that is ready for harvest, ready to nourish whoever comes by.

Yes, God has plowed the soil of my life with hardships like Momma's death, and I realize He takes His time bringing forth the crop only He can identify, a crop He knows will flourish.

As I close the story we've just shared, I pray that you have been encouraged to be brave, to not give up, to trust that trustworthy God … no matter what.

CHAPTER 8

A CONVERSATION IN THE AFTERMATH

About a month or so after burying Mom, I was staring into a cup of coffee, my heart and mind still numb from the trauma of all that had happened. Suddenly the thought popped into my head as if I were reading it on a computer screen: "You are mad at Me because I let your mother drown, aren't you?"

I wasn't startled; I knew Who was asking me the question.

In my mind I replied, "As a matter of fact, now that You mention it, I am angry! Momma had always feared drowning, and that was how You let her die." Up until that moment, I had not even thought about this.

New thoughts began to come: "Other than trying to breathe, did your momma thrash around as if she were afraid?" I thought about those last moments and had to answer, "No, she didn't."

"You also thought you were holding her at the end, and you felt all alone. But I was the One holding her" came the words across the screen of my mind. Picturing Jesus holding Momma was a comfort.

The conversation continued: "You are angry because you didn't hear any angelic singing or smell any heavenly fragrance or see any heavenly lights. You are angry because the moment of Melrose's death felt so dark and desolate, not comforting or affirming or joyous like some other Christians have said they experienced when a loved one passed."

Once again I pondered these thoughts that I had not previously entertained. My response surprised me, "You're right! I speak to people all over the world, and I would have told everyone if I had experienced anything like that when Momma died. I was doing my best to let her know I was glad she was going to heaven."

By this time I was trembling. "Yet I didn't experience anything but wrenching anguish! Why, God?" I knew I was conversing with God because I would have never have come up with the response that was about to come.

"And you would have been on *Oprah*!"

"Yes! And I would have told everyone I met! Many people would have heard about Your presence at Momma's death."

What God said to me next stilled my whole body. "RoseAnne, I didn't want you to spend the rest of your life talking about your mother's death. I want you to tell the story of My love for others by teaching the Bible, by telling others what you see of Me in everyday, ordinary moments. Besides, did I come for you the morning of January 23?"

With a sheepish grin, I replied that He had not come for me.

"RoseAnne, when I come for you, I promise you will get the whole show!"

Even now as I remember what I received from God that day, I realize that, over the years, Momma's dying has brought me to a deeper level of living, that the raging fire of grief and sorrow about our separation has burned away some of the fluff and fears in my heart. Although I still need healing in many areas, I have grown through the anguish of this terrible separation from my mother. I am learning that God is more trustworthy than we could have ever imagined. You can trust him, too.

CHAPTER 9

I STAND ON HER SHOULDERS

I loved going to Nannie and Papa's little white farmhouse in Huntsville, Alabama. There were always delicious things to eat, and I always got a special present: a cowboy kerchief, a toy rifle, hair clasps, new shoes, store-bought ice cream in a sugar cone, or whatever else Papa and I could think to buy.

Papa and Nannie also had stories to fill the time I visited with them. Often Nannie talked about World War II. One of the topics that often came up was the four years of rationing. Nannie remembered wearing cotton socks because silk stockings were either not to be found or too expensive for paychecks like Nannie and Papa's.

When I asked if she minded wearing cotton socks, Nannie got this look in her eyes that always came when she was remembering the hard days of the past. Speaking softly with her distinctive Tennessee accent, my grandmother answered, "RoseAnne, we had to endure a lot harder things than wearing cotton socks. But we didn't mind because we were all doing what we could to help win the War! What I sacrificed was nothing like the soldiers were going through. You know, Uncle Lavonne was in the Battle of the Bulge, and it was so-o-o-o hard on him. Why, we have no idea just how terrible it was for him. He came back with a case of bad nerves. No, wearing cotton socks wasn't a sacrifice, but it was a hardship."

WILLING TO SACRIFICE

Some research filled in the holes of my memories about

rationing. I looked on the website MrDonn.org that the definition of rationing is "a system that provided everyone with the same amount of scarce goods." Many items—like tires, cars, bicycles, gas, fuel oil and kerosene, solid fuel, stoves, shoes, and typewriters—became scarce because they were needed to supply the military. Also rationed were processed foods, meat, canned fish, cheese, canned milk, and fats. Sugar and coffee were extremely scarce, because they were brought to the U.S. by ship from other countries.

"Oh, darlin', I missed sugar and coffee! Sometimes I wanted coffee so bad, I could just taste it! After the war, I would put some grounds in my mouth to chew. I was just so hungry for the taste of coffee and so proud I could buy it again!"

Nannie talked about her ration book filled with stamps about half the size of a postage stamp. Although her groceries still cost money, Nannie had to have the ration stamps in order to purchase the things she needed. Each week the merchants would post what the ration stamps would buy, and that was all there was.

I once bought a ration booklet at an antique store for a few dollars. Many of these leftover stamps had the word *sugar* printed on them, indicating that this commodity was hardly available to purchase even if someone had the money to spend. On the back of the ration book were printed these words:

Rationing is a vital part of your country's war effort. Any attempt to violate the rules in an effort to deny someone his share will create hardship and help the enemy.

This book is your Government's assurance of your right to buy your share of certain goods made scarce by war. Price ceilings have also been established for your protection. Dealers must post these prices conspicuously. Don't pay more.

Give your whole support to rationing and thereby conserve our vital goods. Be guided by the rule: "If you don't need it, DON'T BUY IT."

As I read the government's guidelines, explanations, and exhortations to each American citizen, I understood more about Nannie's courageous and ingenious response to hardship. Yes, rationing made life very difficult, but life had almost always been difficult for Nannie. She had wanted to go to college and major in English, because she loved writing, poetry, and expressing her opinions in essays. She never gave up her dream to one day be a published author. Ten years after her death and in these pages, Nannie's dream has come true—and she would say her section is the best part of this book. (Marie never suffered from a lack of self-confidence!)

First, though, here is a little geography lesson to help you know where Nannie's stories are set. She was born and raised in a little town called Pelham, Tennessee, a rural hamlet east of Murfreesboro and close to Monteagle Mountain. When my grandmother Marie was little, the only modes of transportation were wagons, buggies, horses, mules, and human feet. Life was hard for most families; they scraped by and barely survived.

Marie was the oldest daughter and second child. She had five brothers and one sister, and she worked like a servant for her mother. Marie had little time for play, but her phenomenal memory for details made her an excellent storyteller.

REMEMBERING THE PAST

At the age of seventy-six, Nannie had Momma buy her a handheld cassette recorder and some blank tapes. She would sit in her rocker in the carport and record detailed memories and stories—and preach some sermons, too. I want to share some of these memories because Marie paints a picture of a time and a way of life long gone—but the picture is essential to knowing the dirt from which I spring.

PRAYERS ARE GIFTS WE GIVE TO CHILDREN

"I started to school in 1915. We lived close to the Methodist parsonage in Pelham, so many of those dear people would lay their hands on this little cotton top of mine and ask God to bless me. I realized that out there somewhere was a big God. I was not hardly old enough to know what it was all about, but I had confidence that these who loved me and asked the blessings on me knew that real God. He still exists today. Sometimes we don't remind the children of their protection in the world as they go out, and how they must worship and serve this true and living God."

MARIE'S TENDER HEART

"We had a children's day at church, and the leaders would give us recitations to say. We had very few colored people in Pelham, but one of them was washing for us. Bea told me that her daughter, Ruth Pearl, had the same piece to recite as I did, but she didn't have nothing to wear. My mother had this black taffeta dress that had about four widths in the skirt and was real long, and Ruth Pearl was very big. Well, as I always say, I tried to use what I had to help somebody else—and yet it wasn't mine to use. I cut up my mother's Sunday dress to make one for Ruth Pearl. I burned the scraps under the kettle while Bea was boiling the clothes. When she got ready to go home, she had a dress for her daughter to wear that coming Sunday.

"Somehow our neighbor, Sister Green, found out about the new dress and said, 'Marie, you shouldn't have done that! Your mother won't be able to go to church.' She wasn't the only one who thought what I did was terrible, and I guess it was. But to me, I was just trying to help somebody who needed help, even if it took my mother's Sunday dress.

"Well, Sunday came and nobody said anything about anything. All of us went to Sunday school. My mother came for preaching, but we only had preaching once a month. When my mother was getting ready to come, she couldn't find her Sunday dress. Finally, she went over to Sister Green's and said, 'I can't find my Sunday dress, so you will just have to go without me.'

"Miss Green said, 'I hate to be the one to tell you, Miss Jones, but you won't find that Sunday dress unless you go to the colored people's Children's Day today. Ruth Pearl will have your Sunday dress on.'

"My momma said, 'What?!'

"She replied, 'Yes, Marie took your dress and made Ruth Pearl a dress so she would have a nice outfit to wear, because Marie couldn't stand the thought of her having the same speech she had recited, but have no dress to wear.'

"Everyone thought it was terrible, and you know, it was; but on the other hand I'd cut up nearly anything today to help somebody else. So, it was not a lesson for me to think that I shouldn't have cut up Momma's dress, because I did what I felt needed to be done. I think Momma was mad that she had made me make my own clothes!"

MONEY MANAGEMENT ADVICE

"Although he didn't have much—didn't nobody have much—Papa might give us a dime to spend on ice cream. We couldn't wait to spend our dime. Children are the same today: if they got something, they can't be happy until they get shed of it, especially if it's money. After they get what the money will buy, they might want a little more money. But there's more in circulation today than there was in our time. We knew when we spent our dimes, that was it, and we weren't going to get another dime. But most children today don't know that, because those of us who are older and went without, want to give them more money. That's not good for them or us. We need to be more careful of how we teach the children to spend their dimes."

THE IMPORTANCE OF LEARNING

"Papa knew how important an education was. He got his education on his own. I can remember him getting up at 3:00 in the morning and studying until daylight. Then he'd go out to his little crop of gardens and work until time to open up a little store he had there in Pelham. How many people today would do that?"

MA JONES: QUICK MIND, SHARP TONGUE

"People always helped those in need. The night that I finished high school, coming down the mountain, we had a flat tire. A man stopped and said to my mother, 'Oh, we've had a wedding,' because I had my white graduation dress on. My mother said, 'No, we've had a flat tire.'"

DOING WHAT NEEDED TO BE DONE

Because of all the difficulties she experienced in her young life, Dora Marie Jones knew who she was, and she believed she could accomplish whatever she made up her mind to do. She was a strong woman, unafraid of hard work, and that was a good thing.

Since her mother had decided that her oldest daughter had to help at home raising the other children, Marie was not given the opportunity to go to college. But she borrowed books from two old-maid sisters who lived up the road, and she would read by oil-lamplight after she finished all her chores. Reading stories of world adventure, my grandmother realized that she wanted more than to stay in Tracy City all her life. Her dream was to go to college, major in English, and be a writer.

This unfulfilled dream is why Marie was determined that her children would go to college and, later, that her grandchildren would attend as well. Once while I was attending Samford University, Nannie sent a tuition check made out to the university, and on the memo line she wrote only "RoseAnne." One of the ladies in accounting called me to tell me. It was good I was the only RoseAnne on campus! I called my grandmother to see what she had been thinking and to say that what she had done had not been a wise thing to do and what would have happened if the woman in accounting had not known me. I'll never forget Nannie's answer: "Well, RoseAnne, everybody knows your Nannie."

Marie married Arthur L. Bibles and had one child who lived, my mother, Melrose. Papa's heart was weakened by the childhood fever and, later, by smoking. So Papa didn't do much physical work, and Nannie had to take up the slack: she cooked, cleaned, gardened, canned, and cared for the cows and the chickens on their small farm.

Nannie would fuss about Papa's volunteering to help: "Yes, Arthur loves to volunteer to help! He tells people not to worry, that he will get whatever it is done. Well, I'll tell you the truth: Arthur volunteers, but Marie gets the job done!" Papa would laugh—and Nannie would fume.

SERVING ONE'S COUNTRY

I recently found a copy of a page from the 1943 Sears, Roebuck and Company catalogue. It had a drawing of a farmer with a pitchfork in his hands and a barn behind him. These were the words written underneath:

Soldier Without Uniform

You also serve—you who stand behind the plow, pledged to feed the Soldier, the Worker, the Ally, and, with God's help, all the hungry victims of this war!

You also serve—you who farm, you who pray and sacrifice. You'll feed the World even if it means plowing by lantern light, and harvesting by hand—even children's hands—even if it means putting up the trucks and going back to covered wagons once again.

You are Pioneers once more, with the best land on the globe to fight for—to keep free, and the best tools on earth with which to do the job.

You also serve—and America salutes you—not for stars like a General's pinned on your shoulders—but for the stars you'll help keep in our flag and in the clean sky overhead!

PRODUCE MORE FOOD FOR FREEDOM

Underneath was this message:

> The U. S. Department of Agriculture Urges You to:
> See your County USDA War Board
> Meet your 1943 farm goals
> Keep tractors working
> Take good care of your machinery
> Conserve your trucks
> Turn in your scrap
> Buy War Bonds
> Farmers must win the Battle of the Land with the machinery they already have.

Encouragement like this is what kept my mother's parents working, sacrificing, and living on as little as possible to help the war effort, to support the soldiers, and to make the world a better place for their daughter and her children.

THEY PLANT AGAIN

Arthur, Marie, and Melrose Bibles—and many unnamed Americans in the country and in the cities—met the challenge of their day, fed the troops, and went without sugar and coffee and butter and gas and cars and tires and cheese and meat and heating fuel and cooking fat and rubber products and food that they could have kept for their own hungry bellies and to meet their own needs and wants.

There was no Coca-Cola produced during the Second World War because of the scarcity of sugar. There was no candy production during the Second World War because of the scarcity of sugar. There were no coffee stands during the Second World War because of the scarcity of coffee. When I learned that, I understood why my Papa Bibles always wanted those little ten-cent bottles of ice-cold Coca-Cola in his refrigerator to drink whenever he pleased!

The industry of Nannie and Papa's generation reminds me of the people I saw in Nairobi, Kenya, digging and planting the seeds of collard-like greens (the dietary staple) in every available piece of dirt beside the roads, in the ditches, and along the footpaths to the bus stops. While visiting a sorority sister who had lived with her husband and two daughters in Kenya for over twenty years, I asked Jennifer, "What happens to what is planted in land they do not own?"

Risking only a quick glance away from the crazy Nairobi traffic, Jennifer replied, "The government usually comes right behind them and digs it all up."

Thinking about how discouraged I would be, I said, "What do the people do next?"

In the voice of a woman used to seeing many hungry people, Jennifer said, "What anyone would do if their children are hungry: they come behind the crews and plant again."

My mother's mother, Dora Marie Jones Bibles, was an excellent example of that kind of mother—and of the women of the World War II era. She was industrious and frugal, going without so that others could have enough. She was up at 3:30 in the morning to get her housework done before the sun rose, so that she could then be outside working in the garden to tend and gather. She would prepare and cook the vegetables for lunch as well as for the supper pails she and Papa took to the mill to eat during their second-shift job. She was a spool spinner and he, a supervisor.

The Stories I Keep

NO BIRDS, NO GOSSIP, NO FARM

Nannie and Papa were faithful God-followers.

Nannie would walk to church with her tithe of a dime held tightly in her hand for fear of losing this farmer/mill worker's equivalent of the biblical widow's mite. And long after Papa died of a heart attack at age fifty-four, I discovered that my mother's parents had taken out a second mortgage in order to give their church money to build a house for God in their little community of mill workers.

Despite the 3:30 a.m. start to her day and its 10:00 p.m. endpoint, Nannie still had the energy and time to sit in the front-porch rocker, hold her blond-haired granddaughter, and happily tell stories of her family and sing hymns and songs like "Red River Valley" and "Hang Down Your Head, Tom Dooley." Nannie said we were singing to the birds, but my grandmother couldn't sing very well. She didn't seem to notice that the birds didn't come.

Nannie didn't abide gossip, foul language, or sass, but she did tell me if I ever got in jail, to call her. She wouldn't come, she explained, but she would send someone—and then she would crack that side-of-her-face grin, the only acknowledgment of her sharp wit. She made it very clear that any unlawful activity was for other people's children. I realized that a judge's sentence to serve time would be preferable to breaking my Nannie's heart or bringing shame on the people who had done so much to help me be who I was and have what I had.

Another piece of family history that I didn't hear discussed until I was older was the fact that Papa's father lost the family farm in a card game. Several days later, Mr. Bibles was admitted to the state mental hospital in Tuscaloosa, Alabama. No one could say for sure if he was actually mentally unstable or just too scared to go home.

A FAMILY LEGACY

So there are no Nobel Prize winners in my family. Just farmers, teachers, politicians, grocers, librarians, and mill workers. For folks like my family, the rhythm of daily life was much like a 4/4 beat. They had learned this time signature from their parents and their grandparents: the life music of those generations was one note to one beat, four notes to one day's measure. They would work hard, live simply; live simply, work hard. These people knew well the value of possessions, both personal and family, because they knew the high cost in time, physical labor, and cash.

Despite these values and due in part to death and debt, there was no Coleman family land to inherit, and so with a doctorate in English, I am paying on a farm of a half-acre of land and growing tomatoes, crowder peas, okra, pole beans, zinnias, and dahlias. Before she died, I asked my grandmother to teach me how to grow things, but she refused because she didn't want me to ruin my hands. Motivated by her own unfulfilled dreams, Nannie had sacrificed in order to educate my mother and then my mother's two girls so that we would be able to use our brains more than our bodies as Nannie had had to do. So today I am learning to grow vegetables by reading and watching others—and I wear gloves ... sometimes.

When Nannie's last living sibling died, I was told that the Hamby green bean Ma Jones's people had developed had not been saved, because no one had a garden anymore. I had watched Nannie carefully preserve starter seeds from each year's crop so she could have the same green bean on her table that her family had been eating for almost one hundred years.

Gone.

Now in the second half of my life, I am trying to keep up with the Joneses—with Nannie's people—but I am having to slow down and strip down to do so. I am trying to live life in a 4/4 time as opposed to the 12/4 time I had been living for much of my life. Trying to cram 12 beats into the space of four notes can certainly hinder one's efforts to grow a life bearing the true riches of trust, love and contentment.

I am trying to grow enough food for myself and for others. I want to learn how to "put up" what I grow in order to reduce my need for outside food sources. I want to search the hollows of Monteagle Mountain, find the Hamby green bean, and then grow a hundred bushels a year.

I am a woman from a long line of women who have had to learn how to survive, who know how to sacrifice, who know how to share. I am who I am because my mother was who she was because my grandmother was who she was.

In her later years, I would ask Nannie how she was doing.

Her reply was always the same: "Doing the best I can with what I've got." I am learning to do the same.

One thing more: Whose are you? What do you have to pass on? To whom will you pass that baton?

The future really does depend on your answer.

Answer well.

CHAPTER 10

JUST A GLASS OF WATER

My Nannie loved the colors of fall—gold, orange, brown—but they were not my favorites. Her birthday was in September, but she said she would have loved that season anyway. Since she loved fall colors, Nannie used them in her house, in the clothes she made for herself, and in the clothes she made for me. My mother's mother loved me more than the moon, but she would not abide my passionate declaration, "I hate orange and gold!"

Because she was my grandmother, because she paid hard-earned money for the material and thread and any appliquéd extras, and because she spent hours to help defray clothing costs for my parents, I wore many articles of clothing that screamed, "My grandmother made this, and my mother made me wear it!"

In sharp contrast, on my father's side of the family, Grandmama Coleman purchased me fancy dresses from the exclusive children's clothing store in Sylacauga, Alabama. My father's mother wouldn't dream of sending me something homemade. After all, her grandfather had owned a plantation and fought in the Act of Northern Aggression (the Civil War, to all non-Southerners), and just because he sold the land before they found the largest deposit of marble didn't mean squat when it came to the worth of her family. They weren't rich, but they should have been.

AN INTERESTING WOMAN

As far as I can remember, my paternal grandmother's opinion was the trump card in every area of life. Mabel Elizabeth

Caudle Coleman was an interesting woman. Case in point.

Right after marrying my grandfather, his parents invited the newlyweds to their house to eat supper. My grandmother stated in no uncertain terms that she didn't want to eat supper with them, but my grandfather hadn't yet been schooled in the precision of her word choices. My grandfather, a handsome guy with an easy laugh, adored his wife and would do anything for her, and he assumed the reciprocal was true.

That evening my grandfather had his first lesson in Mabel: she meant what she said. When he opened her car door at his parents' house, she refused to get out. Mabel simply reiterated that she did not want to eat with his parents. Although my great-grandfather was one of the finest marble carvers in the area (most of his work could be found in the cemetery), Jesse Coleman was also a known drinker—"drunk" was the word I would hear from her in later years—and she didn't want to eat at his table.

The story goes that when he couldn't coax his bride out of the vehicle, Grandfather told her to do what she wanted, and he went into the house. I guess she did what she wanted, because she never left the car the entire time that dinner was served and eaten, dishes were washed and put away.

I guess there is something to be said for standing your ground. However, whenever I followed Mabel's example in my world, I was severely whipped for being rude, uppity, disobedient, and rebellious. It didn't matter that Grandmama acted the same way.

A BIRTHDAY DINNER

My birthday is April 13, and hers was April 15. One year on a school night, Dad wanted to drive from Gadsden to Grandmama's house in Sylacauga to take her out to eat a birthday dinner at a catfish place right on the river in Childersburg. When Dad told his mother of his plans, she told him she didn't want to eat at a catfish place on the river, so not to drive the three-hour round trip to take her. My dad almost never responded to whatever his mother said; the game was to ignore the words and do the opposite. Doing what was unsaid was the surest way to win the game. So, responding as if he hadn't heard the menacing tone of her stone-cold words, Dad said it was no trouble for us to come to celebrate on her special day.

To my ear, their phone call was only happy and kind. The unheard responses, however, made Dad dig in his heels and hope that once we got there—once she saw the only family besides my uncle she would have anything to do with, once she felt the love we would bring in by the carload—Grandmama would tell him how much she appreciated his not listening to her.

With God as my witness, Grandmama told Dad—and Momma, Sherry, and me—in no uncertain terms just how much she appreciated not being heard or obeyed. Dad told Sherry and me to go first, thinking the mere sight of her granddaughters would melt the woman's heart.

Because Sherry was young and sickly, she wasn't always held responsible for being obedient and compliant. I, as the firstborn, had to go first or pay the price. When I saw Grandmama's face through the door, the spastic colon I had developed early in life twisted with the anxiety that came with tackling a responsibility too large: my colon was absorbing the impact of a hurricane in order to grant time so those inland could formulate a response. I was trapped: the storm of rage threatening in front, denial blocking the rear.

NO WARM WELCOME HERE

When Grandmama opened the front door, the welcome went something like this.

First there was an awkward silence, broken by the sound of the venetian blinds on the front door banging back and forth as she jerked open the door.

A whispered command came from the rear: "Say something."

"Hey, Grandmama. Happy birthday!"

Isn't a hug defined as a joint effort? Well, I put my arms around an unresponsive woman and put my lips to the turned cheek that had been offered to me emotionlessly. I could smell the makeup powder she constantly applied to abate the sweating of her face. Instead of being a comforting smell, that scent affected me more like gunpowder.

"I told you not to come, Jimmy."

"Kiss Grandmama, Sherry." I'm not sure how my dad thought Sherry would do that since the old woman didn't bow down to her little granddaughter's level.

"Happy Birthday, Grandmama!" said my mother, whom Grandmama had never accepted as good enough to marry her firstborn son, whom she had planned on retaining a long time so he would continue caring for her. It didn't seem possible, but Grandmama stiffened even more with the embrace and kiss of her only daughter-in-law.

I don't remember the mother/son reunion, because I had already escaped into the den where the television was.

In fact, I don't remember anything else until we were ordering our food.

"Well, Mother," said Dad in an upbeat I-know-you-are-pleased-we-drove-all-this-way-on-a-weeknight-to-honor-the-day-of-your-birth tone.

"Jimmy," she said in the same tone used to say the name *Hitler*, "I told you not to drive all the way over here with the girls!" To the waitress, she said: "Miss, just bring me a glass of water."

By this time I felt like the Radio City Rockettes were doing the high kicks of their grand finale in my spastic colon. Grandmama might not have to eat anything, but I would have to swallow each bite while the tension was as taut as fence wire.

Dad was heh-hehing like someone staring down the barrel of a locked and loaded shotgun: "Oh, Momma, surely you want something to eat! We've driven all this way so you could eat catfish on your birthday!"

Grandmama said in no uncertain terms, "*I told you I did not want to go to the catfish restaurant for my birthday and that you had better not come!*"

My mother, as she witnessed this crushing of her husband's heart under the high heel of his cold-blooded you-had-better-do-as-I-say-or-else mother, looked up at the waitress and said with a slight shake of her head and a tight smile: "Ma'am, why don't you give us a few more minutes?"

NUCLEAR-FAMILY FUSION

I learned about the distribution of energy from such times of celebration with my father's mother. Here's the lesson: when two sources of intense heat collide, the fire that has burned the longest and the hottest sucks the oxygen from the smaller, younger one, threatening every time to snuff him out—offspring or no. However, to my dad's credit, he never let the severe burns that came with every encounter deter his trying.

The waitress approached our table like someone inching up to a bomb with a faulty timer. In the accent of someone who lived in some rural section of Talledega County, the brave, young woman looked at my grandmother and asked, "Whaddayahave, ma'am?"

"Water" was the stiff reply.

"Yes, ma'am. You already have your water. What would you like to eat?" the waitress asked, hoping that the water she had already provided the old, blue-haired woman would count for something.

"I said I wanted water, and that is all!" Grandmama snapped.

The girl's eyes widened at the threatening tone of the woman who seemed—at least from a distance—the picture of Southern belle.

"No problem," the waitress wisely affirmed.

"Now, Momma! You have to have more than just water! It's your birthday, and we drove all the way from Gadsden and now to Childersburg to this special catfish place right on the river! Get the catfish platter!" my dad said to the side of his mother's face, since she would not look at him.

"Jimmy," Grandmama said with her voice rising and her tone steely, "I told you not to come, I told you I did not want to come, and now I am telling you that all I want is water!"

My father looked at his mother for just a second, his face flashing with the myriad of emotions running through his mind and heart.

"She'll have the catfish platter," Dad said to the waitress who had now taken a few steps back in case the storm brewing on the old woman's face started throwing lightning bolts in the same way that her daddy's Chevy truck threw a rod last summer.

The blue-haired woman's face turned to stone, a hardening process that had started in the heart and moved up.

"I will not eat a bite." My father's mother emphasized every word. It seemed to me that the only thing Grandmama was going to chew up was her son's good intentions.

THE HISTORY OF THE ICE QUEEN

My grandmother's maiden name was Caudle, supposedly of Scottish origin. Her sister, Lucille, did a genealogy project and declared that our line went back to James Monroe, but she never let anyone actually see the information.

Lucille's emotional state was mercurial. She might invite you out to her house to visit, but by the time you started to pull in the driveway, she would be standing on her front porch, holding a double-barreled shotgun, and wanting to know who the hell you were and what the hell you were doing on her property—and I'm just quoting, not cussing.

No family Sunday lunches at Lucille's house.

Although a wee bit south of stable, my great aunt did have a terrific sense of humor, and all three of the Caudle sisters—Ruby, Mabel, and Lucille—had a most delightful, infectious, and recognizable laughter. The sound came from their bellies, causing them to tightly close their already almond-shaped eyelids, and soon tears that somehow squeezed through the corners necessitated their dabbing with the ever-present handkerchief or, in later years, tissues.

With such an ability to laugh and make others laugh, one would have thought that Grandmama would have been more agreeable and fun to be with.

Wrong.

A HARD LIFE

It is true that Mabel had had a hard life. Grandfather wanted to attend Moody Bible Institute in Chicago, Illinois, where he also worked full-time for Montgomery Ward. Illinois was far away from family for this Alabama girl, and life was quite difficult for the wife and now mother of two boys, especially since she had little money for taking care of the family's needs. Although they had just barely enough canned vegetable soup for dinner, Alf—as my paternal grandfather was called—would usually bring home a stranger who had nowhere else to eat.

Alf felt that God was leading him—and therefore his family—out west to take a better position with Montgomery Ward, as well as serve as a pastor of a church. In a few of the photos that remain from their time in Denver, Alf and Mable are laughing. Even when they aren't, he seemed to have a smile just under the surface.

All had gone well in Denver, and Alf considered his next career step. He interviewed to serve as the dean of men and an instructor at Fuller Theological Seminary in California. However, a week before he was to visit the Fuller campus to tie up loose ends, Alf was driving Jimmy—his eldest son and my father—to school. It was the first day in January after the holidays.

Just a few blocks from their house, a man was distracted by a large airplane, ran a red light, and rammed into the driver's side of Grandfather's car. The impact threw my grandfather out of the car, killing him instantly, and crushed the car's chassis around my dad in the passenger's seat, injuring him only slightly. A witness who testified at the coroner's inquest stated that she saw a young boy running down the street, yelling, "Somebody help my daddy! Somebody help my daddy!"

Although Alf had made his wife promise to stay in Denver where there were kind and caring men who would help her raise the boys if something should happen to him, Mable shipped her husband's body back to Sylacauga to be buried—and she moved her family back as well.

FAMILY SECRETS

I do not have consistent memories of Grandmama before I was in grade school. Only snippets here and there.

In about 1958 or 1959, we celebrated Christmas at her house in Alexander City, Alabama, and Santa brought me a harmonica. Its sharp edge cut the corner of my mouth as I tried to play it the way I had seen it done on the television. And it's still visible. The scar from the cut, that is.

I accidentally punched a hole in my mother's wool sweater that was hanging on one of the posts of my grandmother's poster bed when I was climbing it like a tree.

I remember a Mason jar of Confederate paper money on the steps going to the basement.

I ate a meal with Momma, Dad, Grandmama, Uncle Bobby (Dad's younger brother), and a man I didn't recognize. Maybe I don't actually remember the meal but instead just saw the pictures through the years and finally asked Momma who that strange man was. Even as an adult I was shocked to hear he was one of my grandmother's three husbands. I had only known about the first.

We never had a Coleman or a Caudle family reunion, and I don't remember any holiday we celebrated at Grandmama's house where her two sisters and their families came over to eat or open presents or just visit—and they lived only miles away. Grandmama's only brother lived in Mississippi, and I met him just once—at her funeral.

Another revelation at her funeral was meeting Grandfather's sister, our great aunt, who lived in Hueytown, Alabama, which was just twenty minutes or so from the first teaching job I had. I had lived in Birmingham for twelve years, but no one had ever told my sister or me that we had a blood relation nearby.

Grandmama didn't want us to know about Grandfather's family. (Remember that she didn't even get out of the car to eat supper with them right after she had married Alf.) And she didn't really want us to know about her family either.

NOT A HAPPY CATFISH DINNER

I wish I could report that the catfish birthday party had a happy ending. Nope.

With an untouched plate of catfish in front of her, Grandmama sat silently, sipping her water, while my family tried to act as if this was a normal birthday celebration, not the insane situation in which we actually found ourselves. Not only did she not touch her food, but Grandmama refused to open any of the presents we had brought. Dad opened them for her, commenting on how much she would like the perfume and whatever else Mother had bought.

As Sherry grew up, she was—and still is—a shrewd judge of people and an uncanny predictor of their actions. (She also has what we call "It," which Nannie and Momma had, too. These three would have dreams about things that came true. That happens to Sherry, but not to me. I only dream I'm in Wal-Mart with no clothes on.) Sherry predicted that when we cleaned out Grandmama's house after her death, we would find many of the presents we had given her over the years still unopened, untouched, and obviously unused. And that Sherry—she was right on the money … or on the presents.

Grandmama gave us the same "present" every Thanksgiving

and Christmas holiday. I remember how Grandmama played the game: agreeing to come to our house, calling the day before to say she just couldn't come that year, and then making my dad beg her to come either during that same call or else in however many calls it took until she "changed her mind." When she finally did arrive, she would be cool and reserved, looking out from underneath her hooded eyes like a judge who had already decided that everything and everyone was beneath her.

It is amazingly sad how little I know about my paternal grandmother—but I know enough. For Grandmama's sake, I hope God has been able to make her happy since she has passed on, because she sure as heck wasn't happy with us.

Amen.

CHAPTER 11

TOO GOOD TO BE TRUE

I am not a savvy businesswoman. What looks like a great deal to me usually loses money. I would like to learn how to make better business choices, and I certainly would not mind having enough money to buy more land to plant food crops.

So, when my friend V received a personal invitation through the mail to attend a seminar that would offer an extraordinary business opportunity for her and one other person and she chose me to be that other person, I jumped. We were not obligated to purchase anything, and the clincher for me was that the sponsors were so sure of their product that they would provide a free lunch Saturday and a free electronic organizer to all who stayed for the whole day-and-a-half presentation.

Throughout the sessions, we saw DVD clips of men and women who had secured their financial future just by buying and operating three or more websites purchased at a seminar like the one we were attending. One couple had made over a million dollars in a single year, and we were told over and over that they had raked in that amount by selling "wheat grass seeds, a plastic tub, and ten pounds of dirt."

God may hold the patent on creating seeds and dirt, but a husband and wife from the Midwest are collecting the royalties. To think we live in a country where folks like us might become millionaires by selling a sack of dirt! I wondered how people could be sucked into thinking that someone else's dirt is better than their own?

REDEFINING ART VIA THE WEB

During our breaks we were encouraged to think of both the good we could do with a portion of our soon-to-be-earned profits and the fun we could have with the money that would appear every month like manna in the desert—and we would only have to work a few hours a week if we could find a product to offer and then make folks believe they needed it.

V and I were also fortunate to hear from a man who had been in a seminar just like ours several years earlier. Upon the seminar's invitation, he cleared his schedule and flew in to tell us about his successful ventures. One of his six-plus websites sold statues of fairies and trolls for yards and flower gardens. Who could have known that so many people would be googling for exactly that product!

It does seem, though, that we have moved quite a distance in our statuary tastes from artists such as Michelangelo or Rodin. The work of such masters made the human heart leap with grief or passion with their lifelike masterpieces carved from a block of cold stone, many of which have survived invasions, bombings during the World Wars, and, more recently, floods.

However, today we must be seeing the art of the future in this demand for concrete images of trolls and fairies that also will not succumb to the ravages of time, not to mention Weed Eaters. I guess a successful businessperson can predict the trend and give customers what they want.

A VISION'S IMPACT ON POLITICS

Honestly, I experienced a moment of envy, wishing I had the seminar presenter's vision, his gift, his ability to foresee a nation's need. And I found myself thinking of the first televised presidential debates between the dashing John F. Kennedy and the dumpy Richard Nixon. I don't know if Kennedy had the epiphany or not, but someone realized that a little bit of makeup could go a long way in helping a nation choose the next leader of the Free World.

One cannot forget what America had endured with the no-nonsense, I-do-not-give-a-damn-what-you-think-of-me attitude of Harry S. Truman from Missouri. Looking back on the past few leaders of the Free World, the younger Democratic nominee of the

1960 presidential race apparently could foresee and therefore offer us what we did not even know we needed: a handsome, debonair President who looked so dashing that we had to listen to him on the radio in order to stay focused enough to learn his platform.

Also, JFK had a beautiful First Lady who was as appealing and mysterious as any queen could be. Remember, it had not been too many years since America had the stand-in First Lady in the Truman White House: his daughter, Margaret, although the salt of the earth, hopefully had an inner beauty since the media referred to her as a plain-looking girl who thought she could sing. Evidently, her father also thought she could sing and put her on the radio so the entire world could judge the cultural taste of the man whom the American people had elected as the moderator of the Senate, not the President of the United States.

But I digress.

AN IRRESISTIBLE OPPORTUNITY

Sitting in the business seminar, I wondered if the purchase of these websites could usher in the Age of Camelot in my life, enabling me to become wealthy by providing consumers with goods that might not be included in their wills but could quite possibly bridge—in the world of yard art—the gap, metaphorically speaking, between Truman by succession and Kennedy by choice.

My friend and I drew closer to the campfire, built by those who offered to broker a treaty between our dreams and our reality and thereby bring us lasting peace and contentment. This looked like a smart investment. Actually, it looked like one we would be foolish to refuse. We discussed what we would do while we ate our free lunch, served by veteran waiters and waitresses, and had our first look at our free electronic organizers, a $75.00 value, although I thought I had seen the same one at Big Lots for $10. Guess I was mistaken.

The moment of truth arrived with a surprise. Because we had been in the seminar, we had the opportunity to purchase three sites, and that amazing offer came complete with a year of twenty-four-hour customer service: we would have full-time access to someone who could help us design and launch each site as well as provide suggestions and encouragement. Furthermore, if we really wanted to dream big, we could buy six websites for the seminar special—but only for the next two hours.

The blood started pounding in my ears as my thoughts rushed around and crashed against one another in my brain. If I could get even one site working and producing profit, I could begin to pay off my house loan and maybe even help my family with immediate needs like reliable vehicles for work and much-needed repairs for their houses before their homes began to deteriorate beyond help. Besides, I have always wanted to help others in need, even people outside my family. That was the heritage passed on by my mother and her family.

Maybe this purchase could also bring in funds to set up, in my mother's memory, a scholarship in biology at her college in Alabama. That would be one way I could keep her memory and her name alive.

So my friend and I decided to invest in something that we could not see. We decided to invest in ourselves and in our future in hopes of accomplishing many good things.

YOUR OWN PRIVATE SEMINAR

A year and a half later, I am now inviting you to a mini–seminar. It starts immediately, and it will take only a wee bit of your time. For no extra cost to you, I will share some wisdom I have gained that just may change your life:

There is no free lunch.
Choose substance over looks.
Work hard to be content with what you have.
Those who take advantage of others will taste the salt of the weaker ones' tears and the wrath of God who sees all.

Thanks for attending my seminar—and have a nice day.

The Stories I Keep

CHAPTER 12

LOVE CAN MELT A STONE

Until my mother died, I didn't think much about coffins or cemetery plots or gravestone markers. I had also never considered how little space a tombstone affords for an adequate description of a person's life. There were so many great things to say about Momma that we could have bought many plots, put up several large memorial stones, and stated at the end of each stone's inscription "See next stone."

Looking at the graves around Momma's, I've read things like "Rest in peace," "Called home," "Beloved mother," and "Gone but not forgotten." It may be my dark humor, but I can't help wondering if anyone has ever told the whole truth about the departed one, like "A bitter woman," "A constant complainer," "Good riddance," or a Southerner's "With Jesus—Bless His Heart."

My friend Tricia and her sister, however, put the perfect words on their mother's grave marker: "I have fought the good fight, I have finished the course, I have kept the faith." They could have put no better description on the tombstone of Marie Farr Walker, or "Mom Walker," as we all called her. She was as tenacious as Kipling's mongoose when she was fighting for what she deemed right. She was a brilliant and charming negotiator, always finding the best price for materials and regularly sweet-talking workers and craftsmen into helping her finish many ambitious projects. Mom Walker had the gift of sensing beauty under layers of paint, varnish, mud, decay, anger, hurt, and hopelessness.

She saw through mine.

MOM LOVED JESUS

Marie grew to be a faithful follower of her Lord, growing wiser and learning to love in the same way Christ loved her, living as one who knew Jesus well enough to know where the key to the back door was hidden. Many church people go to God's house every Sunday but stay in the front room like strangers. They never go to the kitchen where true relationship happens as the food is prepared and then served by loving hands in holy communion.

My spiritual hero, Miss Helen Wright, always said that love is the most powerful force in the universe. In an interview on *The CBS Sunday Morning Show*, the songwriter and singer James Taylor said much the same thing when asked how he had overcome his downward spiral of self-destruction. I'll never forget his answer: "Unconditional love on a daily basis can melt a stone" (December 23, 2007).

Even after her death, Marie's life spoke of the powerful truth that one person can make a difference, that a cup of water given to a thirsty soul does change the world—one cup, one person, one stone at a time.

Oh, my friend, our world is desperate for a drink of that sacred water.

MELTING THE STONE OF PREJUDICE

Edith Marie Farr was born on July 19, 1918, in Harriston, Mississippi, a little railroad town two miles from the county seat of Fayette. Her mother—or "mutha," as she pronounced it— was Edith, and her "deddy" was J. V. Farr. J. V. was a section foreman for the Illinois-Central Railroad, making him responsible for maintaining a certain segment of track, and all the members of his work crew—called a section gang—were African American men.

Years later Marie wrote, "The men called Deddy 'Cap'em,' not as master and servant as [some] would picture it. My deddy worked and sweated as hard on that railroad gang as did his men. The 'captain' was an expression of love and respect."[1] Although the Farr family followed the socially acceptable black/white mores of their society, Marie learned that the only people to be held in contempt were the ones—black, white, or any other color—who expected to have a living provided for them without working for anything themselves.

The Stories I Keep

The man in Mr. Farr's section gang who chanted and sang to keep the group working together in rhythm was Charlie Jerome Selman. Just "Jelly" to most folks. Marie and Jelly were friends for almost fifty years. The pair met when she was a child. Jelly was helping lay a concrete walk from her house's back steps to the outdoor kitchen where her mother washed. Jelly had on a new pair of khaki pants, and concrete splashed on them. Marie could tell by Jelly's expression that this was probably his only pair of pants, so she cried and cried for him because her heart was so tender. From that moment on, she named Jelly as one of her favorite people.

Another event brought the little white girl and the black man even closer. It happened the day Mr. Farr let his two sons and daughter ride on a railroad push car loaded with crossties. One of the crossties was sticking out and hit a milepost sign. Mr. Farr was able to grab his two boys, but lacking a third hand, he wasn't able to grab his little Marie. She ended up at the bottom of the pile.

Recounting the story, Marie said, "I can still see Jelly, throwing crossties off me like they were toothpicks and then carrying me all the way to the house, me screaming the whole way, more scared than hurt." Many years later, Marie said that in a way they were worlds apart, but she would have done anything to help Jelly and did many, many times—and over the years he helped her when she needed him.

Then came the Great Depression. Mr. Farr planted a larger crop of vegetables to help feed his family as well as his men. He was deeply committed to taking care of the men who worked for him every day. A great example of that commitment happened the day that another section gang was allowed to unload some freight cars in the rail yard, robbing Mr. Farr's men of their pay. J. V. went home from work, took down a revolver from his closet shelf, and then walked into town to the depot. Placing the .44 on the railroad agent's desk, the section boss said quietly and calmly, "My men are starving. They are going to unload those cars." The next morning they did—with Jelly's singing out the cadence on an empty stomach.

As the years passed, Jelly took to drinking. One night he got drunk and got into a fight. As he passed by the Farrs' house on the way to jail, Jelly cried out, "Cap'em, Cap'em, please don't let them take me away! They will beat me." Mr. Farr said, "No, I won't let them. Now you go on to jail." Marie said at the moment all four of J. V. and Edith's children started crying and "kept it up." Early the next morning, Papa Dear (as his grandchildren came to call J. V.) was at the jail to retrieve the now sober man.

In a tribute she wrote a week after her old friend's death, Mom Walker declared, "You can bet your bottom dollar no one touched Jelly that night."

The day before J. V. died, he imagined Jelly standing in his hospital room, an indication of just how much he cared for that man. On the day of J. V.'s funeral, the black men waited on the hill of the cemetery until the white mourners had gone. Then the section gang gathered around their beloved leader one last time, placing on the grave the only thing they could afford: a pinecone wreath. Marie kept that wreath, a symbol of sacrifice and love that melted the stone of prejudice.

JUST WHITTLIN'

Marie Farr married James Monroe Walker on October 24, 1940, at the First Baptist Church of Jackson with only a few witnesses and some candles. They couldn't afford a car, so someone had to give them a ride to the train station. They went to New Orleans for their $75 honeymoon. Angela was born in 1945 and Tricia in 1952. In late 1956 Jimmie and Marie bought the antebellum home Secluseval. The house had not been maintained for many years and was about to fall to ruin. This was a project that suited Marie to a T.

In 1958, Mr. Walker came home for lunch and announced that he had just purchased *The Fayette Chronicle*, the small town's weekly newspaper. He then informed Marie that she was the new editor. Although not trained in journalism, Mom Walker successfully ran the paper until 1980.

Each week Marie wrote a column called "Just Whittlin'," in honor of her daddy who went to the courthouse every Saturday morning to sit and whittle with other old men who gathered there. The column was where she spoke her mind, shared her thoughts, and introduced new ideas. You see, not everything in Marie's world, in her South, revolved around the black-white issue. There were those—and she was among them—who honored everyone, no matter the skin color, and treated all the same. As I said in an earlier chapter, my childhood didn't include hate talk against those different from us. I didn't know anything about the Klan until I was in college. Not all things Southern are damnable.

A FESTERING WOUND

It would be absurd to define Marie Walker as a white supremacist who wanted the blacks to "stay in their place," who didn't want them to have equal rights. That was not her heart at all. In fact, far from hating black people, most Southerners interacted with African Americans on many levels, even working side by side. It was not the day-to-day activities but the unspoken social laws that kept the boundary between the races clear.

It doesn't seem much different from how ethnic neighborhoods have operated in New York City: Italians in Little Italy, Orientals in Chinatown, everyone keeping to his own part of town. Though such separation could eventually promote prejudice, for many it was just life as they had always known it. People outside their ethnic group were not familiar, so social interaction with them was uncomfortable.

And that was the case for Marie Walker's generation and the one before her. Babies were born into a world with the laws—unspoken as well as written—already established. Most folks' lives were full with taking care of families and farms, using the little money and limited resources they had. Small churches couldn't afford to hire a full time preacher, so worshippers went to whatever church had a preacher that Sunday—no matter their denomination of choice. Life had holidays and Sundays for visiting with relatives. Most people did the best they could with what they had. Many people never even thought of ostracizing someone whose skin color was different from their own. They just wanted life to remain as steady and predictable as possible; they didn't want to take on anyone else's problems.

No matter how one tries to explain it, though, there is still no valid explanation for denying African Americans—or women—their civil rights. And a rage still stalked the land, its roots in the Civil War and the Reconstruction afterward. This rage was not ethereal, so it could not just dissipate like a mist on the water. This rage had a life of its own; it had built walls of separation and blown up bridges of communication. This deep anger had woven itself into the political and social arenas of human relationships. Like the treatment of a festering wound, a deep cut would have to be made to release the pressure.

The time of cutting was drawing near.

THE SOUTH HEATS UP

Unsuccessful in his personal bid to be governor of Mississippi, Jimmie Walker was campaign manager for John Bell Williams, who served as governor from 1968-1972 and was known as one of the most vocal segregationalists, in line with Alabama's governor George C. Wallace. During this time, tension was building in Mississippi.

Although her husband was a recognizable politician on the state level, Marie was the one thrust into the national spotlight in 1969 when Charles Evers, the brother of murdered civil rights leader Medgar Evers, became a candidate for the mayor of Fayette. Prior to this, much had already happened in Mississippi to attract worldwide attention: in the late 1950s the NAACP came in to register more blacks to vote; in August 1961 Marion Barry held workshops to teach young blacks nonviolent protest methods; in June 1963 Medgar Evers was shot and killed by an unknown gunman in the driveway of his home. The gunman was later identified as Byron de la Beckwith, who was convicted after three trials and thirty years had passed.

Although Charles shared his brother's commitment to civil rights for blacks, he was by his own admission an entrepreneur committed to making a lot of money by legal—and admittedly illegal—activities. Therefore, on merely an ideological basis (which was far from the only point on which they were at odds), Charles Evers and Marie Walker were destined for conflict. Charles was known to say that she was his worst enemy. Marie and her newspaper proved to be a great irritant to Mr. Evers. After all, she had her eagle eye trained on him, and she wrote about what she saw.

Evers's campaign drew the eyes of the world to Mississippi, to the little town of Fayette, and to the little newspaper and its editor, Marie Walker. It was said that, at one point, there were as many reporters and correspondents in town as there were citizens. Charles Evers won the election on May 14, 1969, and the news media repeatedly said he was the first black mayor of a biracial town in the South since Reconstruction.

After Evers was declared the winner, a CBS Evening News reporter stopped Marie on the street and asked, "Do you think people around here will resent the fact that they have a Negro for a mayor?" It's interesting to watch the actual television footage and see Mom Walker's face as she formulated an answer for the waiting world. Here was a woman who had lived and operated according to the "separate but equal" boundary lines observed in the South, but she now faced a changing world.

Mrs. Walker could have said many truthful and disturbing things about the newly elected mayor. She could have rightly stated that Charles didn't know the first thing about leading the town. Marie could have spoken about her own desire to keep things the way she had known all her life.

But she did not. After hesitating for a few seconds, the daughter of J. V. and Edith Farr answered, "Some of them will—and some of them are going to wait to see what he can do and give him that chance."

Make no mistake. The following years were not easy ones for Charles or Marie. The two sparred many times over many issues. The educational publisher McGraw-Hill even produced a filmstrip featuring the adversaries presenting their perspectives on the racial debate. It was entitled "Fayette: A Study in Black and White."

By 1972 when Jimmie Walker, then the excise commissioner for the state of Mississippi, succumbed to cancer, it was evident that things had begun to change for the better between Mr. Evers and Mrs. Walker. As Mr. Walker's funeral procession passed through Fayette from Jackson, the family was surprised to see all the flags in Fayette lowered to half-mast in honor and memory of Jimmie Walker—at the order of Mayor Evers.

James Taylor said it correctly: Love can melt a stone.

JOINING HANDS
Marie began to look closely at the poor and unem-

ployed in Fayette and Jefferson County. She was disgusted with a welfare system that pays poor people to stay poor, unemployed, and birthing numerous babies. She could not abide the laziness of many of the citizens who believed that the federal government should be responsible for providing them with money and food stamps without their working at all. The Walkers were better off economically than some in Fayette, but both Jimmie and Marie worked hard for what they had—and they taught their daughters to do the same, just as their parents and grandparents had done.

After leaving *The Fayette Chronicle*, Marie had more time to reflect on how her parents had raised her and on what she believed God said in the Bible about loving one's neighbors. As the years passed, Charles and Marie, two former adversaries, eventually began to work together to try to help the residents of Fayette have a better life and to give their children some hope for the future. Mr. Evers and Mrs. Walker became like a pair of old horses going to work in the fields for the good of others. Charles was then heard to say, "Mrs. Walker is my worst enemy—and my best friend."

Love can melt a stone.

HOMEGOING

Early in December 1993, Marie Walker had spent the day supervising the hanging of the town's Christmas decorations on Main Street. That evening, while talking on the phone with a friend, she suffered a heart attack. When Angela, her daughter, couldn't revive her, she called Will T. to come help her. Will T. was a black man Mom had hired to help with the massive amount of upkeep required by the family's fixer-upper antebellum home.

On a historical note, Jefferson Davis was the first house-guest. One time Tricia, Mom's youngest daughter, brought a girl from Brooklyn to stay at Secluseval for a weekend. As her older sister Angela led the visitor to the bedroom where a Confederate uniform is displayed in a glass case, she said with great pride, "Jefferson Davis was the first guest to spend the night here." The Yankee looked puzzled and asked, "Who's that?" I'm not sure the girl was ever invited back.

When Will T. saw that the front gate was closed and therefore locked, he didn't even slow down, crashing his truck through the wooden fence beside the gate, not thinking about damage to either his truck or the fence, so intent was he to get to Mrs. Walker. He was too late, though. Mom Walker had died.

About a year before Mrs. Walker passed, Will T. had been singing the Missionary Baptist hymn "He'll Understand and Say Well Done" as they worked on some project. Marie said, "Will T., I want you to sing that at my funeral." There had been another man working with them that day, and after Mrs. Walker died, he reminded Will T. of her request.

"Aw, she was just kidding," Will T. told the man.

The other man replied, "Naw. Miz Walker don't kid."

In addition to that request, Mom had also wanted Will T. to build her a simple casket of oak, lined with satin. Over and over she had told him to take her measurements so he could start and finish the project before it was needed.

But thinking of making Mrs. Walker's casket before she was dead spooked Will T., so he would never even talk about it with her. But when she died that Sunday night, Will T. went home and began right away to fulfill his friend's wish. He worked around the clock—crying the whole time—until he delivered the box to the funeral home. Just like her daddy, Marie loved and respected those who were around her, and they loved and respected her in return.

LONG TIME A-COMIN'

The day of the funeral dawned clear and warm in southern Mississippi. Not once in her life did Mom Walker preach; instead, she taught by example. This day was no different. For the first time in Fayette, three black men and three white men joined together to carry their friend's casket—and Will T. was one of them.

Tricia asked if I would perform her mother's funeral, so the minister of the local Methodist church and I led the procession out of the restored, stately house. Our somber parade filed between the white, Doric columns and down the porch steps, silent except for the heavy breathing of the pallbearers as they struggled over uneven ground in the afternoon heat.

As we began to walk toward the family graveyard, the smell of freshly dug dirt floated toward us on the breeze, as did the sound of a black gospel quartet (minus one who couldn't come) singing

"The Rough Side of the Mountain."

As we walked noisily over the dry, dead leaves, I remember thinking, "This seems surreal, like I'm in a movie about the South a hundred years ago." However, as I took my place under the tent just a few feet from the yawning red grave, a cold chill snapped me back to reality: we were not reliving history; we were making it.

If the service had been held in the Methodist church or at a public cemetery, it would have been like J. V. Farr's funeral: the blacks would have stood away from the whites, waiting for their turn to pay their respects and say good-bye to their friend. At Mom's funeral—and in a great tribute to a woman who had exhibited the depth of character to embrace former adversaries as friends—black and white, friend and enemy, stood intermingled on the same, level ground.

As I finished my part of the service, I asked if anyone had some final words to say about Marie Walker. Former Mayor Charles Evers, also a pallbearer, was the first one to speak honoring and respectful words about the woman who had become his friend. "I have lost my dearest friend," he said, his voice cracking with grief. "Our community has lost its dearest friend. Marie Walker taught us how to live together and love one another."

Helen Hunter, one of Mom's friends, then spoke up: "When there was work to be done, Marie was the first one to pick up the shevel (shovel)."

A few others spoke aloud, and the crowd murmured its assent as others talked about Mrs. Walker.

Finally Will T. fulfilled his friend's request. Stepping from his place as a pallbearer, he began to sing the final song, "He'll Understand and Say Well Done." And I was struck anew by the significance of the scene before me.

Death is no respecter of persons, no matter race or ideology or theology. God knows our shortcomings and weaknesses, our sins of the heart against others and ourselves. The Lord knew what was in Marie Walker's heart and life just as He knows yours and mine. That's why we frail beings find hope in the Lord's power to help us change. We also find peace in His mercy: without it, no one could ever stand before Him, for no one is sinless.

My throat tightened as I saw the evidence of change, of progress, of mercy, and of hope for the future. Hot tears flowed from hearts that once had been hard as a stone but now were soft enough to bond together those willing to pick up the shovel Mom Walker had left behind for them.

There were no television reporters or cameras recording this historic event. There were no fireworks here, no shouted words or shaken fists fueled by the molten lava of an internal volcano of frustration, fear, anger, or hate. That kind of negative news is what makes stations number one at five, six, or ten o'clock.

Evidently the media was only interested in the explosion, but they didn't care to stay involved in the story. They didn't report on these people's struggle for understanding, nor did they publicize healing and what these people accomplished *together*. On the day of Mom Walker's funeral, there was no blood spilled; just tears. On that day there were no angry words; just voices filled with honor and respect for their fallen friend.

One newspaper reporter was present for the funeral, but Bernie Sheahan was there as a friend. In her article "The Homecoming," in December 8, 1994, edition of the *Nashville Scene*, this weekly columnist wrote that Mom Walker liked Old Milwaukee beer in the can. Sheahan also told of something else Mom enjoyed: "'Miss Bernie,' she'd say some evenings, 'I think it's time for a toddy, don't you?'"

There is still prejudice here in the South, but much of it has nothing to do with skin color. Instead, it has to do with denominations of churches. So, some who hear this story will not care one whit about Marie Walker's courageous actions to help others and build bridges between people. Instead, these folks will cast judgment because of beer in the can, a hot toddy, and a woman's conducting a funeral. That will be all they remember and talk about. And that's too bad.

HE'LL SAY, "WELL DONE"

I remember my last visit with Mom Walker just months before she died. We were sitting in rocking chairs on the side porch of her daughter Tricia's 1850 Cheatham County farmhouse that they had salvaged and restored. Across the way I could see the log cabin that was also being redone.

As we sat together and I looked at her rocking back and forth, I saw the lines on her face not as wrinkles from age but as badges of honor adorning one who had met life head on and stood her ground. Mom said, "Miss RoseAnne, only recently have I learned just not to worry about things or people like I did for years. I now know that God has everything under control, and He will work everything out."

Mom stopped rocking, looked straight into my eyes, and said, "I have more peace than I have ever known. Now, tell me what's going on with you."

Today let's raise our glasses in memory and honor of a woman short of stature who decided to take big strides toward reconciliation for the sake of love. Here is a toast that my friend Bernie Sheahan taught us at one of Tricia's birthday celebrations:

> Here's to us
> Who's like us
> Damn few
> And they're all dead!

I salute you, Mom Walker, and I bless the Mississippi ground that holds you until we all will be in the Presence of the Love that melts the stone.

Come quickly, Lord Jesus.

CHAPTER 13

THE CAT
WHISPERER

Several years ago I saw a black cat crossing the field to the northeast of my house. Her dark coat made her stand out as if against snow instead of grass. I called out to the animal, "Hey, Black Kitty!" She stopped immediately, turning toward the sound of my voice. After a moment of standing motionless, the cat continued her deliberate course.

In the following months, I saw the stray crossing the fields on both sides of Rose Hill. As with many relationships, I do not remember the exact moment when the shift happened, but one day when I was going to the barn, the feline was closer to the fence than she had ever come. I decided to try my hand as a cat whisperer. I sat down on the driveway and began to say, "Hey, Black Kitty." To my amazement, she answered with a "M-rau-ow," reminding me of a Siamese's elongated response.

For the better part of an hour, I said, "Hey, Black Kitty," to which she responded, "M-rau-ow." With each verbal interaction, Black Kitty came closer and closer to me. Finally, she was near enough to touch. For a long while, we both just sat in amicable silence as, inch by inch, I slowly moved my arm toward the animal.

Finally, the cat allowed me to stroke her gleaming black back. I was stunned when she began to purr so loudly that she seemed to vibrate. After a while, Black Kitty rose and walked back the way she had come. In the following weeks, I put out dry food as a welcome, and she began to come every day to eat. I would rub her back while she ate, but she didn't seem to want to be touched very long.

Now it is four years later. After the arrival of this first guest, two other cats came to Rose Hill, and we were one big happy family: Black Kitty, Tigger (sickly from his arrival), Joe Louis (his stocky build and short legs made him look like a boxer), Miss Millie (a Lhasa I bought as a seven-week-old puppy at the side of the interstate in Austin, Texas), and me (a stray myself). Unfortunately, last summer Joe Louis developed a stomach tumor, and I had to put him to sleep.

I returned from Russia a month after having lost Joe. To my shock, I realized Tigger was sick when I opened the back door and he didn't even move. Tigger had been my constant companion whenever I worked outside. He would keep his distance until the sun began to set, and then he would sit at my side until I went into the house to put out wet food for all the felines. To see him so close to death was heart wrenching.

Williamson County Veterinarian Clinic put my feline buddy in intensive care for twenty-four hours, but to no avail. With my friends Valerie and Shirley at my side, I held Tigger as the vet gave him the shot that took him out of his misery. I cannot put into words the grief that fell with the tears that wet my sweet companion's fur.

CHATTING WITH BLACK KITTY

With both males gone, I was afraid for Black Kitty. The temperatures were plunging below freezing, and she was now alone. So I brought her into the house to spend the night. At daybreak, she woke me up with her very loud "M-rau-o-w-w-w" to go outside. We did this for several days until I set up a litter box that Black Kitty learned to use in three days. Amazing for an old, stray cat.

One day I heard her familiar cry come faintly from the other side of the house. As a joke to myself, I said, "What, Black Kitty?" But the joke was on me because she answered, "M-rraauu-ouww!" We called back and forth, with her response going up in pitch and volume each time, until she sauntered into the room. I quipped, "Well, there you are, Black Kitty," to which she replied, while cutting her eyes and moving her head almost in a shrug, "M-RAU-raow" in a much lower pitch and volume. She absolutely knew what I had said, and she responded with a cat's seeming indifference. After all, she had called for me first. I picked her up and petted the silky smooth, gleaming black fur on her body and the soft white fur on her chest and belly.

Other times, Black Kitty will call out, locate me, and then come just to be in the same room with me, just to sit on the carpet near my desk chair. My presence must be enough because soon her loud, vibrating purr starts, and she is obviously fully content. How cool is this stray, the one someone threw out, the one whose back leg someone hurt, the one who decided to take a chance to trust a two-legged creature—and still she seeks me out, even though I accidentally step on her tail or trip over her in the kitchen

Black Kitty talks to me quite frequently when she's in the house. And when she is outside and I come home in the car, she will meet me on the driveway, and she's talking already. We have worked out a system. I stop next to her, pick her up, put her in my lap, and then drive to where I park. My feline friend sits perfectly still for the short ride, purring like a racing motor. This has become another regular custom for us, an unexpected "Welcome Home" initiated by a cat.

Hoo-boy—I know there must be someone thinking, "This chick has lost her cluck." However, God has been kind enough to bring me creatures great and small who talk, if you will allow me to use that word, because being single all my life means there are many periods of silence in my days, broken up by my conversations with the animals. And let me tell you, they have said some very funny things.

Okay.

LEARNING FROM BLACK KITTY

Black Kitty found me in the bathroom this morning. She knows to call for me, to listen, and then to come to the one who will pet, then feed, and then open the outside door for her. This cat believes and trusts in me—even though she has known abuse, cruelty, and injury at the hands of other humans. I, on the other hand, am a human, supposedly superior in my reasoning and intellectual abilities. However, I am not as smart—or as trusting—as Black Kitty, because I do not call out to my Master to talk with Him, seek Him out so I can curl up in His arms of love, or go to Him just to sit quietly in His presence, satisfied with knowing that I am loved and cared for and worth His attention.

In this arduous journey of life, I do well to listen to the voices of ones wiser than I, ones with much experience on this earthly pilgrimage. One of those voices of wisdom is Oswald Chambers. After his death, his wife Biddy compiled excerpts from her husband's work and published them under the title *My Utmost for His Highest*. The reading for this day on which I was contemplating my unusual companions was called "The Discipline of Difficulty." The day's verse came from the sacred book of John: "In the world you will have tribulation; but be of good cheer; I have overcome the world" (16:33).

Here were words spoken by Jesus, the Son of God, centuries ago; words recorded by John just a few years later; words taught by Mr. Chambers in the nineteenth century; and words unbelievably applicable to my specific troubles in this present year. The commentary could not have been more specific and relevant if dear Oswald had been sitting with me:

> An average view of the Christian life is that it means it is deliverance from trouble. It is deliverance in trouble, which is very different … If you are a child of God, there certainly will be troubles to meet, but Jesus said do not be surprised when they come … God does not give us overcoming life: He gives us life as we overcome. The strain is the strength. If there is no strain, there is no strength. Are you asking God to give you life and liberty and joy? He cannot, unless you will accept the strain. Immediately you face the strain, you will get the strength.[1]

Here I am reminded that trials will come and stretch me, but God is present. I must, however, seek Him; I must cry out for Him—just as Black Kitty did when she came looking for me today. She wanted to be in my presence because she knew what she would find, what she would receive, and how her needs would be met.

If Black Kitty knows I will care for her, why do I habitually forget to go to God who is always listening for me to call to Him, waiting for me to come into His presence, wanting to meet my every need? It is time I learned this lesson from—a cat.

Okay.

M-rau-o-w-w-w, God?

CHAPTER 14

A GOD WHO RAISES THE ROOF

When I was about five or six, a woman in our small town gave my father a female boxer, and we named her Duchess. One man in our church was a carpenter, and he built a nice house for our new dog. The roof was removable so that we could clean the inside more easily. However, I had a better use for it.

Whenever Duchess had puppies, I would lift the roof of the doghouse, climb in, pull the roof back into place, and sit with the animals. I can still smell the wood shavings that covered the floor—along with the poop. I would pick up each puppy, put it close to my face, feel the ultrasoft fur around the muzzle, kiss the little one's head, and smell that wonderful puppy-breath smell. Duchess was a good mother and would monitor each of her pups so that I wouldn't hurt it. If a little one began to cry, Duchess would nuzzle the puppy until I put it down so she could care for it. I learned early on how comforting and life-giving animals can be.

AN UNEXPECTED COMPANION

After I moved to Nashville, I met a girl who had lost her job. Prior to that, she had told some of us about a dog her family had owned, a Lhasa Apso, an unfamiliar breed to me. When the girl became despondent over her unemployment, several of us bought her a Lhasa puppy.

I kept the puppy for two weeks before we presented her to our friend, who named her Punkin. However, after having the dog for a month, the girl decided she couldn't keep her—and Punkin came home with me.

At first I was a bit put off because I believed my schedule too full to care for a dog. Like most of the other singles I knew, I was almost never home. After all, home was a silent place, empty except for the full-blown echoes of loneliness. So most of us singles ran in packs, together but not really functioning as a stable family. We were all looking for something we didn't have and couldn't find: a healthy, balanced, normal home life.

When I was a child, I had grown familiar with bone-aching loneliness, so I was not surprised to recognize it as an adult. I accepted it unconsciously. Then, unexpectedly, a well-intentioned gift was returned. However, I believe that Punkin was actually a gift intended for such a time as this … for me … from the Almighty.

CHEW TOYS AND CANINE YIPS

Since I was single and teaching only one class a week (with no pay!), I had no reason to get up in the morning. However, that little puppy needed to eat and go outside, and I was the one entrusted with her care. I didn't know that a Lhasa is born for companionship and complete devotion to its master. Now that I had this new bundle of constant energy as my friend, the atmosphere in my house changed. Chew toys and doggy treats were scattered around the hardwood floors, and human laughter and canine yips became the norm, filling up the haunting silence.

Years later, I realized that God had done something for me that was very familiar to me: the Swift, Sure Hand had raised the roof of my life and put a puppy inside with me. Before Punkin's arrival, I had been so depressed that even breathing was a chore. Afterward, every morning was like Christmas as that puppy awakened early and showered me with loving, enthusiastic attention.

HEALING LOVE

For the next ten years, Punkin—along with the wonderful people who decided to be my friends—helped me heal. One of those new friends was Shirley. She would invite Punkin and me over to her house and feed me Campbell's vegetable soup with a piece of toast with melted Muenster, a cheese new to my palate. Pure comfort food!

During those times, Shirley and I realized that we processed information in much the same way. We would spend hours talking about whatever came into our heads. We had similar backgrounds and therefore we told each other familiar stories, but my new friend had experienced walks in this life I had only heard about. I was amazed by her wealth of knowledge and her ability to communicate truth in understandable ways.

Punkin loved visiting the house where Shirley had nannied four children for many years. Shirley said the puppy loved patrolling for crumbs, and the dog found a veritable buffet compared to the slim pickings at home. Actually, Punkin loved Shirley more than crumbs, and that wee pup would go to sleep on a blanket Shirley called "Bear."

I thought nothing of it until one day at lunch the youngest girl Shirley cared for said, "Shirley doesn't touch any other dog except her dog, Patchy. And I can't believe she lets Punkin on her Bear!" At that surprising revelation, I looked at Shirley in shock. She shrugged her shoulders with a cryptic smile that has become familiar.

God had once again lifted the roof of my life and placed another gift inside—a friend whose brain worked much like mine and who had enough kindness in her heart and experience with loneliness to welcome into her life and her heart a wounded woman and her dog. I realized later that Shirley helped to save my life, and I will always be grateful.

DOGS ARE A GIRL'S BEST FRIEND

Everyone who knew me knew Punkin. As this sweet little Lhasa began to age, I realized that we both were slowing down, but it was hard to imagine life without her.

When Momma had a heart attack in January 1998 during treatment for her reoccurring cancer, she had to retire from a teaching career of forty-five years. One day, as I was praying about her being home alone after so many years of being so busy, the message came so clearly that my head snapped up: *Take Punkin to be Momma's company until further notice.*

Although I knew I would miss my dog, I had no doubt that she was to go to Pensacola—and Momma was delighted. Years before when I first brought the new puppy to meet my parents, Mom told me she had always wanted a Lhasa. She laughed with pure joy as the little mop-looking dog ran through the house, gnawed on her finger, and collapsed at her feet in puppy exhaustion.

So when I brought Punkin to stay, there was unspoken communication of appreciation between my mother and me, because she knew how much I loved Punkin. What is even more amazing, Punkin seemed to know that she was there for Momma, and that sweet dog readily became Mom's shadow and couch buddy.

MEET MISS MILLIE

On the Mother's Day weekend after Momma passed in January 1999, I found a seven-week-old Lhasa puppy in Austin, Texas. I named her Miss Millennium Rose of Texas, Miss Millie for short, and she was a three-pound lover. She took to Punkin as if that older dog were her mother. Punkin, however, was highly annoyed by the little ball of fur that delighted in attaching herself under the older dog's chin. Having to fend off the youngster, Punkin seemed to gain a few years' strength. Just as Punkin had done for Momma, Miss Millie gave the old dog companionship, a bit of playfulness, and a good amount of love. Once again it was as if the roof to Punkin's house had been lifted and a gift given to my faithful four-legged friend.

Punkin has been gone for a while now, and Miss Millie is eight years old. She has been even more of a companion to me than Punkin, even more attentive and attached. Whenever I work in the yard, Millie stations herself somewhere nearby, keeping watch over me. Every now and again, she will quietly appear at my side. Sometimes she nuzzles my arm; sometimes she just sits until I notice her presence.

Millie also has the gift of knowing when I'm troubled or angry or hurt, for she will come lie down on my feet or lean her twenty-two pounds against my leg when she senses any angst. The warmth of her little body makes me feel I am not alone, and that's welcome comfort. Having done what she can, Millie then goes to sleep.

A POSTSCRIPT

In that little Lhasa I again see the hand of God caring for me, His created one, in very personal, very situation-specific ways. He reminds me of His love and communicates His desire for connection with me through the very animals He has given me. Some may say this is coincidence; I say that it is God.

The Stories I Keep

CHAPTER 15

REAL HEROES LOVE CHOCOLATE

Unless you just picked up this book and opened right to this page, you know that Roy Rogers was my childhood hero. Now that I am older, though, I find it painfully evident that Dale Evans played a much lesser role than her husband in their television series and movies. Perhaps, then, it's no surprise that among my current TV favorites are shows like *Stargate Atlantis* and *Bones*, where females are important characters who fight evil and have strong friendships with their male counterparts—and the relationships are as important as the battles.

But the people I've mentioned are fictional. Now I want to tell you about someone who was no less a hero than those portrayed on a screen or described in the pages of a novel. Miss Helen Wright is her name, and she was like no one I had ever met. She changed my life, but she was human enough to make me believe I could be like her. Besides that, she l-o-v-e-d chocolate.

Prepare, my friend, to be inspired.

A REAL, LIVE HERO

Once I told Miss Helen Wright that I had two heroes: Roy Rogers and her. Thinking she would be flattered, I was taken aback by her negative response: "Well, it's fine that Roy is, but don't make me a hero!" Despite her objections, when all is said and done— literally, when I consider all that Miss Helen has said and all that she has done—this woman is absolutely my hero.

I met Miss Helen Wright when I was twenty-eight years old.

Before I'd even spent twenty minutes with her, I knew she was like an ancient bard telling stories and bridging the gap between earlier times and the present with tales of victory and defeat, of life and death, of light and darkness, of miraculous deliverance and wisdom deepened through suffering. I wanted to sit at her feet for as long as possible, to listen to her and learn from her.

Some words I read on a card remind me of Miss Helen: "When you come to the edge of all that you know, you must believe in one of two things: There will be earth upon which to stand, or you will be given wings." Helen Wright had experienced both—and she told me I could believe for earth and wings for myself, too. So I walked across the bridge of Miss Helen's words, a bridge that spanned the impossible distance between the crumbling dirt of my life and the holy ground of the God she said knew my name.

AN UNFORGETTABLE SUPPER

I met Miss Helen in 1983 while I was living with three other girls in Homewood, Alabama. I was very busy teaching English at Homewood High School and also working on my master's degree in English at the University of Alabama in Birmingham. My roommate Janet had been spending time with a seventy-four-year-old woman who was a piano instructor at Southeastern Bible College, and Janet wanted to bring this friend to have supper with us.

That's all I needed to hear—the woman was old, and she taught piano at a Bible college. "Thanks, Janet," I told her. "The only thing I have been doing for the past four months is studying for my comprehensive exam. To be honest, I don't have time to have supper with an old woman."

As the daughter of a minister, I had no illusions about the upcoming meeting: I had served my time politely listening to old women's litanies of ailments—their sluggish bowels, their children's woes, their upcoming doctor's appointment. And I was supposed to give up precious study time to be with one more complaining woman? No way!

But my roommate was relentless: "Well, you have to eat, don't you? Then you can go upstairs to study." She had a point.

When the doorbell rang that night, my roommates were

busy with supper preparations, so I was asked to open the door. That ticked me off because the old woman was not my guest. I didn't want to have to be friendly. I just wanted to show up at the table, be introduced, eat my supper, and leave. One-on-one contact with Janet's friend was not part of the deal.

There was a window in our door through which you could normally see the visitor's face, but all I could see was the top of a white head. I thought, *Great. A wrinkly, old woman. That's all I need.* Needless to say, I had preconceived notions about the person I was about to meet.

I drew a deep breath. My momma had trained me to be polite and gracious no matter what, so I brought a smile to my lips. It was fake, but it was there. When I opened the door, there stood a 4'11" woman with a smile stretching from one high cheekbone to the other. A red, knee-length coat revealed two, pencil-thin legs. Our eyes met, and I was struck by their shining blueness.

Before I could spit out the first fake word of my rehearsed greeting, the little lady fired off, "Hey! I'm Helen Wright! Who are you?"

From the very start she was not like any old woman I had ever met. She stood out in the cold for a few moments, because I was too stunned to invite her inside.

By the time we sat down to supper, there was no mistaking it: there was something absolutely and wonderfully different about this woman. First of all, Miss Helen did not act old; second, she didn't tell "old woman" accounts of all her ailments. Instead, she laughed easily and often, and she was entertaining us!

During that meal together, we four young women were spellbound by stories of Miss Helen's everyday life and needs. She explained that, through the words of the Bible and prayer, God had "told" her to pray and ask Him to provide—and then He did just that.

No doubt about it, Miss Helen was extraordinary.

"CAN YOU BEAT THAT?"

At a very young age, Helen Wright began her training as a concert pianist. After graduating from college, she taught for fifteen years at the Conservatory of Music in Birmingham, Alabama (now Birmingham Southern College). During her summer breaks she taught piano at the Interlochen Center for the Arts music camp for gifted young people.

During the 1940s she was a featured pianist with the Alabama Symphony, and she was a well-known concert musician who toured nationally. For many years she invested in her extraordinary natural talent, but then one day God called Miss Helen to leave behind all her success and notoriety.

No retelling does justice to Miss Helen's brilliant spinning of her story, so here are her words:

I was at the beauty parlor, sittin' under the hair dryer, when all of a sudden my heart started goin' POW! POW! POW! I thought I was havin' a heart attack!

But it was just God. He said, "Helen!"—He knows my name!—"Helen, I want you to go straight over to that college, Southeastern. Don't stop at your house, although it's on the way."

God knew my father would not agree with what I was about to do. God said, "I want you to go straight to Southeastern and tell them you're goin' to be their piano teacher."

At first I said, "No!" I was a Methodist, you see, and Southeastern was some kind of weird Bible college. And I wasn't going to go there.

But God said, "Helen!" and my heart went POW! POW! POW! "Helen!"—He hadn't forgotten my name, and He hadn't forgotten what He had suggested a while ago—"I want you to go straight to Southeastern and tell them you are goin' to be their piano teacher."

Well, I told God if He didn't make me have a heart attack, I'd go. And at least He let me get my hair finished!

So I went into the college office in this little building. They didn't really have a campus. They just had a garage and this little building. No piano or music department or anything.

There was this big Swedish woman sitting at a desk, and she scared me to death when she said very abruptly, "What do you wish?" She sounded very irritated with me.

I thought to myself, "Well, I don't wish anything. I don't even know why I'm here!"

But that still, quiet Voice of the Lord said, "Helen, obey Me."

So I said to the woman, "Could you go ask the president if he can meet with me?"

The Swedish secretary said, "As you wish." I don't know why she kept wondering what I was wished. I wished not to be there!

I went into the president's office. He shook my hand and heard my story of the beauty parlor. Then he said, "Miss Wright, I have a story to tell you. Just last night we called a board of directors meeting to pray specifically for a classically trained piano teacher. We prayed that the Lord would send someone whom He would choose, someone who could teach our students classical music, someone who wouldn't care how much money we didn't have, someone who would trust God to provide the need."

I replied, "Well, I'm it!"

Now, I was making a good salary teaching piano at the Conservatory, so I didn't ask how much "not enough money" was. I had prepared all those years to be a concert pianist, and finally, when I was a featured pianist with the Alabama Symphony, God asked me to give it all up to teach piano at a little Bible college that didn't even own a piano or have the money to pay me! But God has provided all that I have needed. Girls, I can say that the Lord is faithful.

Can you beat that?

When Miss Helen asked us four girls, "Can you beat that?" we looked at on another as if to ask, "Would you give up your career and money after a voice 'spoke' to you under a hair dryer?!" But there it was: the question "Can you beat that?" As I looked at this petite, white-haired woman sitting across the table from me, I replied, "No, ma'am, I can't. I can't beat that."

Miss Helen just laughed.

LEARNING OBEDIENCE

In that moment I realized Miss Helen had *not* said, "Now, girls, *you* need to know God just like *I* know Him, and here are the steps *you* need to follow to be just like *me*." She simply told us stories about what had happened and what God had done in her life.

As I compared scenes from my own life to Miss Helen's many stories, all of which held spectacular evidence of God's presence, I thought, *How can she live as she does?*

I was utterly empty compared to Miss Helen Wright.

Furthermore, I had never known anyone like her who trusted God moment by moment—and it sure sounded as if everything had gone well for this woman. However, the next story Miss Helen told us let me know that she, too, had experienced the sharp, cutting edge of personal pain.

Once again, this story is in Miss Helen's words.

I was married many years ago. My parents, my pastor, and everyone who knew me approved of the marriage. However, after several months, he took the Bible engraved with his name, threw it across the room, and said, "I did that to get you!"

I was shocked. I thought God had led me to make this decision. I was known as a committed Christian; I was a Bible study teacher!

And then things went from bad to worse. I became pregnant, and this made my husband very angry. When it came time for our baby to be born, I went to the hospital by myself. During the delivery I was groggy from the ether, but I remember hearing a thud and then a gasp. Someone in the delivery room had dropped my baby. He died three days later. My husband never came to the hospital.

Before this time, I felt God had said to tell only Him about our troubles, about my husband's infidelity. It was humiliating. I would go to the public pool, and my husband would spend time with other women. God began to teach me that He would care for me, no matter what happened.

After the baby died, I told my parents what had been going on in my marriage. They quietly arranged a divorce. There I was: my baby had died, and I was a divorcée. Worst of all, I was afraid all my failures would negatively affect my reputation as a follower of Christ. I was devastated, and I had something like a nervous breakdown.

As we sat around the dining room table and listened to this sad story, I tried to imagine this woman—so strong and full of life as she sat across the table from me—young and in love and full of hope for her future. I just couldn't imagine how I would have felt if I had been deceived by my husband, cheated on, lied to, and then had to deal with the tragic death of my child. Miss Helen had had a complete emotional meltdown after all she'd been through. Could I have even survived that kind of betrayal?

My roommates and I had forgotten to eat. Miss Helen hadn't

eaten more than a mouthful, but we didn't notice until later. I had been on the edge of my seat and so caught up in my own pain that my breathing had become shallow. As I looked into the chasm of my own grief, Miss Helen's next words came as a lifeline as she spoke of God's provision for her.

A friend called me one day to ask my advice about something. I told her she didn't want my advice: I was a divorcée, I was a failure, and I felt that my Christian witness had been destroyed. What my friend said next shocked me. "Helen, before all this happened, you used to say, 'All things work together for good to them that love God, to them who are the called according to his purpose' (Romans 8:28, KJV). I like you a lot better now that I know you have suffered!"

Well, girls, it was true. Before this time I would quote the Bible without fully realizing the depth of other people's pain. I found out for myself that God uses suffering to deepen us and to show us our need of Him. The Bible says that Jesus learned obedience from what He suffered. I was learning the same thing.

What an amazing attitude in the face of great loss!

I had never heard anyone be so honest, so open about her own troubles, her own failures—and then say that Jesus met her right where she was, not where she should have been. I knew my own stories, my own brokenness, my own inability to live the life Miss Helen described, because I did not know Jesus as she obviously did.

I had heard stories of people like Corrie ten Boom who went to a concentration camp because she had helped Jews in World War II and Hudson Taylor who took the love of Christ to previously unreached people in China. Here was a woman, living in my neighborhood, who knew Jesus just like those famous people had. Wow!

BALLET SLIPPERS AND BIRTHDAY CAKES

Miss Helen followed that story by talking about how she needed a bookcase. She prayed that God would show her where to look—and I had never heard of anyone praying about where to find furniture. What she said next broke us all up: "God told me to go to Kmart."

I said incredulously, "God told you to go to *Kmart*?!"

"Yes!" Miss Helen said. "Can you beat that?"

I answered for all of us: "No, ma'am. No, ma'am, I can't."

Even though I thought the stories could not get any more incredible, I was wrong. We served dessert, but Miss Helen's last story was so amazing that I wasn't interested. Miss Helen, however, took a few bites and exclaimed: "I love chocolate!" Wow, real heroes love chocolate.

Some of my piano students at Southeastern taught a Sunday school class at a correctional institution for minors in Chalkville, Alabama. One Sunday their car wouldn't start, so they asked me to drive them there. I ended up taking them that Sunday—and then every Sunday after that for the next year.

Now Chalkville was a very sad place. It was where criminals under the age of eighteen and kids who were abandoned by their families were all put together. I was heartbroken for those kids, but I knew God could touch every heart and life there.

After a year of driving my Southeastern students to their Bible study in Chalkville, they told me they thought I was supposed to teach the class. I said, "What?! I'm not a Bible teacher! I am a piano instructor!"

My students answered, "We think God wants you to teach the Bible too!" So I told the students that if God wanted me to teach the Bible, He would have to tell me Himself. I prayed, "Lord, if You want me to teach the Bible at Chalkville, You have to confirm it."

I went to eat lunch in the college cafeteria, and guess who was there? The president of the college and his wife! We all had lunch together, and I asked their opinion about my teaching the Bible at Chalkville. I couldn't have been more shocked when they both said, "We think you're supposed to do it."

The first Sunday school lesson I taught at Chalkville was from John 14:14 where Jesus says, "If you ask for anything in My name, I will do it." When I finished teaching, I thought I did a great job with those delinquents. Then a girl said, "Miss Helen, I'll ask Jesus to be my Savior if you'll pray for something."

I told that young girl I would, and she said, "I want some red ballet slippers." I said to myself, "Oh no! I forgot to emphasize that Jesus was talking about spiritual things!" But I had just taught that you could pray for anything in His name, and He would hear you. So I told that girl, "Okay. I'll pray." I went straight home and got on my knees and pleaded, "Lord, where can I find red ballet slippers?"

I looked all over Birmingham for those red shoes. I found white, black, and pink—but no red. I returned to Chalkville the next Sunday, and as soon as the little girl saw me, she said, "You ain't been prayin', 'cause I ain't got no red ballet slippers yet!"

I took the little girl aside and said, "I taught it, and it's in the Book. If God doesn't answer, I'm going to resign!"

After I got home, I kneeled by my bed and prayed, "Lord, the little girl asked for red ballet slippers! So if You don't bring them, I'm quitting." Still I could not find red ballet slippers. I returned to Chalkville the next Sunday, fully prepared to tell everyone I wasn't going to teach anymore. As the children came out of their houses to come to Sunday school, I saw that little girl, skipping down the hall toward me, wearing red ballet slippers!

"What?! Where? How?" I exclaimed. "Where did you get those?"

The little girl said, "Why, Miss Helen, don't you know? Jesus gave them to me!"

You know, those red ballet slippers arrived in the mail, addressed to that girl. The package didn't have a postmark or a return address. To this day no one knows who sent those red ballet slippers.

I was so shocked that I kept saying, "What? Where? How?" Finally, the little girl with the red ballet slippers took my hand, walked with me behind the piano, and led herself to the Lord! That girl was my first convert at Chalkville.

Another girl was standing by the piano that day, and she said to me, "I've never had a birthday cake." I sighed with relief and thought to myself, "I can do birthday cakes!" The next week I went and ordered a beautiful cake from the best bakery in Birmingham, and I could hardly wait until Sunday! When I arrived, the little girl saw me standing there with the cake box in my hands and she said, "You didn't trust Jesus would bring me a birthday cake! I've already had three this week!"

I learned an important lesson that day. I needed to pray about everything—even birthday cakes!

FROM MUSIC TEACHER TO MENTOR

Miss Helen had been telling stories for two hours. She

looked at her watch and said she needed to go home. I realized that I hadn't even thought about needing to study. Miss Helen then told us that she had been sick the previous night and all day and almost hadn't come. As the older woman headed for the door, I stumbled for words. "Uh, Miss Helen? Do you think you could teach me piano lessons?"

The Southeastern piano instructor didn't say anything at first, and then she replied, "I'll pray about it."

I was embarrassed. What did she mean, she'd have to pray about it? That was usually a response Christians gave when they were trying to get out of something they didn't want to do, and they used God as their excuse. I thought to myself, *Either you have a lesson opening or you don't! Never mind!*

I forgot about the incident until some time later when I received a small envelope with beautiful and very precise handwriting. I opened it to find a party invitation that said on the front, "We can make beautiful music together." On the inside the word *party* had been whited out and piano *lesson* had been written in. The line identifying "where" read, "Miss Helen's Studio," and the line for "when" said, "At your convenience."

I was stunned. I was going to have one-on-one time with one of the most amazing women I had ever met. It didn't matter that I was paying for the privilege or that I would have to squeeze the time for lessons and practice into my already insane schedule. I didn't care! God had brought Miss Helen to my house, and I had an hour every week to be in her presence.

On the appointed Tuesday afternoon, I went to Miss Helen's studio on the Southeastern Bible College campus to begin my lessons. After we finished my second lesson and I earned my first gold star (I couldn't play at all, so Miss Helen rewarded me as she did her much younger students), she asked me if I would like to hear what God had shown her that day. I shrugged my shoulders and said, "Sure." I was a little hesitant because I had never met anyone who had evidence that she had heard from God, much less that very day.

The small woman invited me to sit across from her at a small, folding table where a 7½" x 12" green-covered book lay open; both pages were filled with writing in black and red ink. As I looked at the words, I asked incredulously, "God showed you all that today?!" With absolutely no hint of spiritual arrogance, Miss Helen replied equally incredulously, "Yes! It's fresh, not canned!"

I never learned to play the piano because after a few weeks I asked Miss Helen if she would be willing to take my lesson time to tell me what Jesus had shown her that day. The piano virtuoso became my spiritual mentor and friend. For the next twenty-two years, Miss Helen taught me about the love of Jesus and walking with Him moment by moment. And she loved me.

MY HERO'S HEROES

It was Miss Helen who introduced me to some of her heroes, to people like Oswald Chambers (*My Utmost for His Highest*), Mrs. Charles Cowman (*Streams in the Desert, Vol. 1*), George Müller, F. B. Meyer, Hannah Whitall Smith, Dr. H. A. Ironside (who led Miss Helen to the Lord), A. B. Simpson, George Matheson, and E. M. Bounds, to name a few. In some respects, time with Helen Wright was like walking through the back of C. S. Lewis's wardrobe into a whole, new world—not a mythical one, but one in which I could truly live.

As I read these authors and sat at the feet of Miss Helen, God worked their words and life examples into the soil of my heart. He provided through them the spiritual organic material that my heart's soil needed to become richer and able to support the seeds of His Word. It was during this time I learned that, although they were tragic and destructive, the difficulties of my life could be used like aged manure. When fresh, manure will burn plants badly and possibly kill them. However, after sitting for a year or so, aged manure is one of the best composts available for encouraging root growth, resulting in healthier plants and more abundant fruit.

Manure is a natural by-product of an animal's life, considered refuse when it is first created but gold after time has aged it. In that sense, manure is a lot like the hardships in my life, whether those hardships came because of others or resulted from my own rebellion or idiocy. The November 16 reading in Mrs. Cowman's *Streams in the Desert, Vol. 1* quotes from an unnamed author:

The greatest things are always hedged about by the hardest things, and we, too, shall find mountains and forests and chariots of iron ... Triumphal arches are not woven out of rose blossoms and silken cords, but of hard blows and bloody scars. The very hardships that you endure in your life today are given by the Master for the explicit purpose of enabling you to win your crown.

Do not wait for some ideal situation ... but rise to meet the actual conditions which the providence of God has placed around you today. Your crown of glory lies embedded in the very heart of these things—those hardships and trials that are pressing you this very hour, week and month of your life.[1]

Before this point, I knew that my life was full of hardships, but now I began to learn that hardships can serve God's purpose for me—if I leaned into them with the Lord's help. Before this time, it was like I used poison to kill the worms I saw in my garden soil, not knowing that a worm's "manure" is the dirt's best friend. Lessons like these can only be taught by those who have gained wisdom from going through the same trials. Ignorance does not have to be deadly.

Read the wisdom of Oswald Chambers:

We mistake the sense of the heroic for being heroes. It is one thing to go through a crisis grandly, but another thing to go through every day glorifying God when there is no witness, no limelight, no one paying the remotest attention to us ... The test of the life of a saint is not success, but faithfulness in human life as it actually is. We will set up success in Christian work as the aim; the aim is to manifest the glory of God in human life, to live the life hid with Christ in God in human conditions.[2]

I have always looked to heroes to show me how to act. Miss Helen, however, was a hero who showed me how to live.

Miss Helen passed her mantle to me, and now, by the grace of God, it is my turn.

Can you beat that?

The Stories I Keep

CHAPTER 16

THE SALT OF THE EARTH

As I mentioned earlier in these pages, I was raised to be an academic in order to be free from what Nannie Bibles, my maternal grandmother, considered a backbreaking life of physical labor. So in ease and comfort, I traveled the road of privilege paved by the sweat and efforts of my grandparents and parents.

Yet, in sifting through the stories remembered and memories misplaced, I made a startling discovery about myself: Every time I look out the window of a plane—whether flying over the United States, Ireland, or Africa—I search for telltale signs of people who live off the land. I have realized that I enjoy speaking for conferences held in large cities and at beautiful resorts, but I absolutely delight in visiting the small towns where I meet farmers who invite me to walk their land with them.

One of my most memorable moments during my trip to Sudan, for instance, occurred after I placed my bags in my thatch-roofed, mud hut and walked to the garden at the back of the compound. Suddenly I spied a familiar plant. I squatted to look more closely at the blossom, and suddenly someone was beside me. I looked into the face of a grinning, dark-skinned man. I smiled back. We needed no introduction: we were people of the soil, and we recognized each other.

When I returned to Russia last year, I saw a couple with whom I had connected the previous year after the man saw pictures of my 1950s International Harvester Cub tractor. They wanted to take me to their home so I could see their garden. So Dr. David

Feick, our translator Katia, and I put our lives into these friends' hands and braved Russian driving. The farm reminded me of something from Tolkien's writings: a small, quaint house with no running water, surrounded on three sides by a garden of flowers and vegetables. As I looked into the eyes of my Russian friends, we all smiled broadly: we were people of the dirt.

Miss Helen had taught me about God and about God's presence in my life. Her death has left a definite void in my days and in my heart. Not only do I miss her amazing stories, but I have missed having an older woman to remind me that when life starts to quake, I need to hang on and hang in. And I'm very aware that I still have much to learn about the dirt and farming, and who would teach me about those things?

Little did I know that my story collection was about to swell with the entrance of a tractor-driving, cattle-raising, bona fide, organic-vegetable-growing, story-telling, strong woman who lives not six miles from my home. God is very funny!

MEETING MRS. E

When I moved into my present house in 2001, someone told me that a relative of Howard and Anita Crunk, the former owners, lived on a farm not too far from me. I also found out that this relative, Elizabeth McCord Crunk, worked at the Garden Center of the Franklin, Tennessee, Kmart.

Kmart. God had told Miss Helen to go there for a bookcase, and Mrs. Elizabeth worked there. Funny.

So I went to the Garden Center to meet Mrs. E, as many call her. We talked for a few minutes, but that was it. She was nice but didn't really seem very impressed with me. Later I found out where her house was. As I drove there, I realized I knew where it was. About a quarter of a mile past her house and barns was a view that was my favorite in the whole area—maybe in the whole world. If I were able to buy land on which to build a house to live in for the rest of my days, I would be ecstatic with any place starting with Mrs. Crunk's house and moving down around the curve for about a mile. I just didn't know that the house, the land, and the amazing view belonged to Mrs. Crunk.

A few years later I was listening to WPLN, the local

National Public Radio station, when I heard Mrs. E's name (pronounced Miz E) and learned that she was signing her land over to the Conservation Easement for the Land of Tennessee that day, ensuring that the many acres of her farm would always remain farmland and never be subdivided. I pulled into her driveway just in time for the ceremony—and, yes, I felt a bit out of place since I had only met Mrs. Elizabeth once.

However, when I reintroduced myself to this eighty-something-year-old cattlewoman as the one living in her brother-in-law's house, Mrs. E remembered me and graciously invited me to see her home, that she had helped build in 1946. As I listened to stories about the construction of the house and the history of different pieces of furniture, I realized that this white-headed lady reminded me of Miss Helen—except for the farming, of course. Miss Helen was like an African violet; Mrs. E was a dirt-dobber.

Although I once saw her on the tractor while she was bush-hogging one of her fields amidst cows and sheep, I didn't visit Mrs. Crunk again until recently. And that visit was prompted when I found in my attic a small, tattered card that had been on a Christmas present, evidently from the 1950s or 1960s. It said, "To: Howard, From: Edwina," and I wondered who *Edwina* was! Obviously not Anita, Howard's *wife*! (I'm not above a little intrigue every now and again.)

All of a sudden, a message flashed across my brain screen: "Go ask Mrs. Elizabeth if she knows who Edwina was." I was ambivalent about going for a visit without having been invited, but I only wanted to remind her who I was and ask my questions. I'd leave right away. So I parked in the gravel driveway of Crunk's Hill View Farm and walked toward the back door of the house. When I was almost to the steps, I saw the white-haired woman in the side yard. She was painting an old, metal lunchbox and leaning on a cane, a new development since I had seen her four years earlier. I also noticed that she was a little more frail.

I called out the older woman's name, but she didn't respond. I continued walking toward her, repeating her name, but she still didn't hear me. But when she did see me, Mrs. Crunk gave me a warm smile and motioned me to her. When I told her my reason for coming, Mrs. E surprised me: "Why, just yesterday I said to myself, 'I wonder if Rose still lives in Howard and Anita's house.'"

How interesting! Years ago God had brought Miss Helen to my house, and that day He led me to Mrs. Crunk's—and He had given her a hint the day before! Mrs. E kept me entertained with story after story, making me totally forget the time. When I looked at my watch, four hours had passed!

From the stories she had kept, I learned that Mrs. Elizabeth has faced many difficult things in her life, many of them occurring after her husband, John Henry Crunk Jr., died suddenly from a heart attack thirty-three years ago, leaving her with forty-five cows to milk twice a day, two at a time, and almost three hundred acres to maintain. She is truly a hero, one who has worked hard to survive and harder to succeed—and she has done both.

A RICH HERITAGE

Elizabeth McCord Crunk's stories are different from Miss Helen's, but they are just as entertaining and enlightening. Like Miss Helen, Mrs. E deserves a hundred pages, and even then I'd just touch the surface of all she has done. A few stories will have to suffice for now.

Elizabeth's people have lived and farmed in this same area of Tennessee for over two hundred years. This fact in itself is astounding to me since the longest I have lived in one geographical area is twenty-three years. Her parents, Walker Leland McCord and Annie Lou Reed McCord, lived with his mother, Laura Ann Walker McCord, in a seventeen-room house. It was originally built for a Baptist couple who attended many large conventions and housed delegates attending those meetings. (In this case, free will must have sold out to predestination, because the McCords were Presbyterians.)

Since his daddy died when he was nine, Walker was very attached to his mother. The story was told that when Mrs. Laura Ann would play the organ at church, Walker and his sister would stand on either side of their mother, holding on to her skirt. He never lived apart from his mother until she died. Although Annie Lou swore she would not live with her mother-in-law, she came to love Mrs. Laura Ann like her own mother. So little Elizabeth had constant access to her amazing grandmother.

Mrs. Laura Ann was a large, capable, tireless woman who ran their Cedar Lane Farm and cared for the family. Some of Elizabeth's earliest memories are of sliding down the mansion's long, winding staircase banister; of her grandmother's pulling her around the house in a red wagon; of their sitting and shelling peas on a big, flat rock in the yard under a locust tree on Saturdays; and of churning butter and preparing hens, both of which were put down into the well to keep cool for Sunday dinner. No matter what the two of them did, Elizabeth loved being with her grandmother, who loved having the little girl with her.

When Elizabeth was four, the big house burned to the ground. The wind was so strong that there weren't even any ashes left; only the iron bed frames and the hams that had been hanging in the attic remained. The hams had been roasted by the flames, and the family ate them thankfully. Mrs. Laura Ann had had the presence of mind to grab her woolen bedspread and throw it out the window, and it was the only thing saved. That bedspread is now hanging in Mrs. E's bedroom with a picture of her grandmother and a loom's shuttle above it. As Mrs. E tells her visitors, "My grandmother raised and sheared the sheep, spun the wool into yarn on the spinning wheel, dyed the yarn, and then wove the bedspread on a loom!"

I was therefore not at all surprised when I asked Elizabeth who was the greatest influence in her life. She quickly replied, "My grandmother. What I learned from her is why I wanted to do what I have done. She was a strong, intelligent woman who accomplished whatever she put her mind to. I also learned from her—and still believe—that we must care for the land."

THE MILITARY WIFE

Walker McCord was a beekeeper, but he did not enjoy farming. In fact, Elizabeth's daddy seemed born to be a carpenter, and he built barns and houses and just about anything else folks needed. When cedar fencing became too expensive and farmers switched to wire, Walker had steady work, because he built fences that were perfectly straight. He was also known for demanding that all bent nails be pulled out, not pounded down. Mrs. E told me that the man who dug her daddy's grave kiddingly said, "Don't you worry. This grave will be square and have no bent nails. I can still hear him say,

'Pull it out, boys!'"

Elizabeth met John Henry Crunk Jr. in high school, and they married in January 1940 on her twenty-first birthday. They bought their farm in March 1943. They built the barn but didn't move into the old house there because Johnnie was drafted, and in September he left for Camp Blandon in Florida. The couple was so much in love that Elizabeth followed him there six weeks later. Her husband had rented her the only space available at the time: the sofa in the living room of a lady's house. She had already rented out her chicken coop, smokehouse, and garage to the wives of other servicemen.

Having little money, Mrs. Crunk would buy one meal at a local diner and divide it into breakfast, lunch, and dinner. Clearly, she needed a job, so every day she stopped at Stumps Department Store to see if Mr. Stump needed help. Eventually her persistence paid off in not only a job at the store, but a job assisting Mr. Stump, who was also the postmaster, sort the heavy mail load coming through Camp Blandon during the war.

One day Johnnie sent word that his division was being shipped out to Fort Meade in Maryland. Thinking they would go by train, he instructed Elizabeth to take the train, so they could be together during the trip. She caught the train, but unfortunately the soldiers left Camp Blandon on buses. When Elizabeth was changing trains in Jacksonville, though, she spied a division of soldiers lined up to board a train to Maryland. With her heart beating rapidly, she began to look for Johnnie in the mass of men. "If I can just see his back, I'll recognize him," she said to herself.

And find him she did! When Johnnie saw his bride out of the corner of his eye, he motioned for Elizabeth to come stand directly behind him. She moved into place and marched right onto the train with all the rest of the soldiers! She wasn't even approached until late that night somewhere in the middle of Georgia.

The conductor tapped Elizabeth on the shoulder and asked, "What are you doing on this train?" When the young woman replied, "Why, I'm going to Fort Meade with my husband!" the conductor replied with a sneer, "Uh-huh, I bet you are!" Realizing that the man thought she was there in a professional capacity, Elizabeth held up her hand with the wedding band and said, "I sure am! See, here's my wedding ring!" Throughout this exchange, she had been poking Johnnie, trying to wake him up to corroborate her story. When he finally woke up, he convinced the conductor that she really was his wife, and no one bothered the young couple the rest of the trip.

But when Elizabeth got off the train in Washington, DC, she had no place to stay. Then she remembered her friend Helen, who worked for the Internal Revenue Service. This twenty-four-year old girl called her friend, who sent her husband, John, to pick her up. The couple found their Tennessee friend a place to live, and John helped Elizabeth get a job where he worked: Julius Garfinkel & Co., then the third largest store in the United States, even bigger than Macy's.

One day while she was working in ready-to-wear, Elizabeth received a call from her friend Helen: "I'm sending a car to pick you up after work because you have to play tennis with Percy Priest [the House representative from Tennessee]." Elizabeth said she didn't want to play tennis with him, but her high-school friend was persistent: "I'm sending a car for you."

So, for as long as she lived in Washington, Elizabeth played tennis with Representative Priest three times a week, helping him prepare for an upcoming tournament. Because of this tennis connection, Percy Priest made it possible for Johnnie to go back to Camp Blandon when the rest of his division went off to Europe. The much-in-love couple had six more weeks together before Johnnie was shipped overseas.

AFTER THE WAR

When Johnnie returned from Europe, the Crunks decided to start a dairy, and they worked their herd up to forty-five Jersey cows. At 4:00 a.m. and 4:00 p.m., Johnnie and Elizabeth fed and milked the cows, at first by hand and later with milking machines that deposited the grade-A milk straight into the holding tank. The milk was picked up every day, providing the hard-working couple with a small paycheck every two weeks.

Life was good—and then Johnnie had a sudden heart attack and died. Her husband's death left the fifty-three-year-old widow with forty-five cows to milk and feed; three thousand pounds of feed to shovel out for the animals each week; and many acres of land to tend. "Early of a morning," Mrs. E remembers, "I would go to the barn at 4:00 to begin milking. My father didn't help, but he would sit outside while I worked. Every day he would tell me to sell the dairy cows, sell the dairy cows. I tried to explain that it was February and I couldn't sell until the fall when the farmers were making their herds."

Mrs. Crunk continued, "One day I finally said, 'Daddy, I'm not a-going to sell the cows until the fall! I'm a-going to make this place work, and I'm going to do it my way!' He said, 'Well, Elizabeth, that's just what I've been waiting to hear! Now I know you're going to be all right.'" Mrs. E did sell the forty-five milk cows, leaving her with forty-five heifers she also needed to sell since money was tight. Then someone she knew called her to ask if she would come to work at the Goose Creek Best Western. She accepted the job, and soon Mrs. Crunk was promoted to manager.

Talk about being in the right place at the right time! When cattle buyers came to the area looking to buy stock, they stayed at the Goose Creek Best Western. Mrs. E worked the crowd and was able to sell the forty-five heifers. Then her daddy gave her five Hereford beef cattle, and Elizabeth began to build her herd. At the time there were only two female farmers in the area, so Mrs. E had to fight against the prejudice even as she dealt with the challenge of running her operation alone.

Then, one Sunday after church, Walker McCord, Elizabeth's dad, went to the barn gate to let the cows in because the temperature was so cold. As he turned back toward the house, he had a heart attack and died. The two men Elizabeth loved most in the world died within eleven months of each other, both from sudden heart attacks. She put a bench between her father's and her husband's graves in the family cemetery. Often she would sit there between them to talk over the problems she was encountering. Not many people know that, though, because it was not Mrs. E's way to tell others about her suffering.

CONFIDENCE AND COURAGE IN THE FACE OF ADVERSITY

Mrs. Crunk was raised to believe in herself and to have the courage to do what needed to be done—no matter the odds or other people's opinions. Two stories illustrate this truth.

When Elizabeth first started her beef-cow herd, the common practice was to allow the bull to roam, so that calves were born year-round. Beef cattle are not like milk cows. Milk cows know to come to the barn, because as they are milked, they are also being fed. Beef cows, however, eat in the fields, so there is no reason for them to come to the barn. Therefore, when calves are born to beef cows in the winter, there is a great chance that the newborns will freeze before they are found.

That's why Mrs. E decided she would breed her heifers so that the calves would be born in the warm fall months. That practice did cut down on the number of calves she could sell, but it also eliminated any deaths due to extreme cold. Many local people made fun of her decision. One man even said, "How you gonna keep them from having calves at that time?!" Mrs. Crunk replied incredulously, "You do know how they are having them, right?" Today in this area, most calves are born in the fall—and it was a good thing for the calves that at least one man discovered how heifers get pregnant.

Another incident that reveals Mrs. E's confidence and intelligence involved pipes and ditches: water was running from a drainage pipe and cutting a deep ditch in one of the pastures. Elizabeth knew that she had to find a way to fill that ditch because the cows could not cross to the other side to graze. One day she saw some huge rocks that had been dug up to clear the way for a building. When the folks told her they didn't know where they could take those rocks, this brilliant woman said, "I know where you can dump them! Right in my ditch." She was surprised, however, to see how many boulders they brought, and she realized they were far too big for her tractor to roll over and work down.

At church the next Sunday, a man walked up to Elizabeth and said, "What in the world do you think you are doing?" Confused, she replied, "I don't know what you're talking about." This church member retorted angrily, "Putting those boulders in that ditch! Now you are going to have two ditches instead of one!"

Out of her mouth popped, "Haven't you ever heard of a sod waterway?" Mrs. E later said that she had no idea where she got those words; they just came out. Then she said to her fellow church member, "And as long as I'm paying the taxes on the land, I can make the water run uphill if I want it to!" She said later that she did know where *those* words came from.

Even with tons of boulders piled up, the ditch needed more filling. So when Mrs. Crunk saw a man digging a pond, she asked him where he was going to haul the dirt. When he said he didn't know, she told him he could dump it in her ditch. Dump he did—forty truckloads. And he brought over his bulldozer to pack down the soil. Then, throughout the winter, she had the hired hands put the round bales of hay in the ditch. The cows could eat what they wanted, and the rest of the hay helped fill the open spaces in the ditch.

Today there actually is a sod waterway that the cows can walk across, just as Mrs. E had envisioned. Although the male church member had been free with his criticism, he was—not surprisingly—stingier with any praise for a job well done. To this day, he has never stopped to congratulate Elizabeth on her success.

TAKING CARE OF BUSINESS

Annie Lou Reed McCord, Elizabeth's mother, lived alone until she was one hundred years old—and until she fell backward down the stairs on her way to quilt. At the time, Elizabeth was working at the Thompson's Station, Tennessee, post office as a mail carrier and then as the postmaster relief. So she would spend the night with her momma and then get up at 4:00 a.m. to be at the post office at 5:00 to start sorting mail. She hired a nurse to be with Annie Lou while she was gone.

When she left the post office at 2:00, Mrs. E had to work at the farm until she went back to her momma's house. When she was just six months shy of qualifying for retirement, her mother said one morning, "Elizabeth, don't go to the post office today," to which Elizabeth replied, "Why, Momma? Who's going to open the door? Who's going to sort the mail?"

Mrs. McCord agreed: "You're right. You need to go on in

to work." Her daughter did go to work, but she quit that afternoon. When asked about not getting retirement after working for fourteen and a half years for the post office, Mrs. E says, "I've never regretted my decision for one moment! Mother and I had a great time together, and I'm glad I was able to be with her the six more months she lived."

When I asked Mrs. E how in the world had she been able to take care of her mom and her farm at the same time, this feisty woman answered, "Anyone could have done what I done, because it was God who gave me health and strength. He has blessed my whole life with health and strength—even when my feet froze when I was riding the horse to school and when the bull broke both my wrists and hurt my back when it charged me while I was getting it out of the pasture with the heifers."

Even with those two exceptions, I heard this lady farmer thanking God for all He had given her. I wondered if, in her situation, I would be grateful for all God had done for me, or would I have been bitter all my days because of the extreme hardships He also allowed?

After Mrs. Annie Lou died, the manager of the Franklin Kmart called Mrs. Crunk: "Elizabeth, I want you to come work in the Garden Center. I need someone who knows the difference between fescue and Bermuda."

So, at the age of seventy-nine, Mrs. E went to work for Kmart, and she stayed for seven years while she was still taking care of forty heifers and bulls. The True Value store in Franklin had been trying to get Mrs. E for their garden department, so she went to work for them when she was eighty-five.

After Mrs. E had been at True Value a year, an ice storm came through the area. Knowing that the potted trees on the lot would be blown over, Elizabeth went into work at 7:00 a.m. Instead of going to the back door as she usually did, she tried to get in the front door because she knew at least two people would be there. The door was locked, however. As the eighty-six-year-old worker was making her way to the back door, she tripped over a brick that was sticking up in the sidewalk and fell on some hoses that had not been rolled up. When Mrs. E tried to stand, she couldn't.

After she had been lying in the parking lot for a time, a truck finally pulled in. Mrs. E asked if he could help her. When he agreed, she told him to go inside and tell the cashier to call 9-1-1. He went into the store and came out with the two employees. When one of them reached to pick her up, Mrs. E said, "Don't touch me! Take this purse over to my truck and get my other purse out, because it has the billfold with my insurance cards in it." Even in great pain, she was one, tough, strong-willed lady.

THE NEXT CHALLENGE

At the hospital, Mrs. Crunk found out that she had broken her right femur and pulled her right hip out of its socket, twisting her leg and tearing ligaments and tendons. When she arrived at the hospital, a niece who is a nurse met her there. The niece spotted Dr. Parsons, an orthopedic surgeon with the Franklin Bone and Joint Clinic, and asked him to look at her aunt. He operated on Mrs. E and put steel plates in the femur and hip to repair some of the damage that one little brick had caused. (Did I mention teeth were knocked out when she fell?)

Mrs. Crunk went to a rehab facility to learn to walk again. When someone cautioned her that she probably wouldn't walk again, "Oh, yes, I *will* walk again!" was her answer. Although her roommate had a television, Mrs. E didn't want one because she was there for one reason and one reason only: to get well. While she was in rehab at eighty-seven years of age, Elizabeth knew she had to face and overcome this obstacle just as she had all the others in her life. She knew the statistics—that older people die within six months to a year after breaking a hip—but she wasn't going to be one of those statistics. After all, she had work to do.

Although her bones were broken and her pain was great, Mrs. Crunk had as sharp a mind as ever. It still didn't take her long to identify a problem and come up with a solution. During rehab, the problem involved pain meds and physical therapy. The morning nurses gave Elizabeth's pain meds around 4:00 or 5:00 a.m., but she would not be taken to therapy until more than four hours had passed—the length of time the drug worked to ease the pain. So one morning Mrs. E refused to take her medicine, raising the ire of the nurse. "I'm not going to take that pill now," she told the nurse. "Let me take it right before they come to get me for therapy, because then it will help ease my pain while I am actually taking physical therapy."

Thinking she was dealing with an old woman who just didn't know what she was talking about, the nurse continued to try to give Mrs. Crunk the medicine. The showdown came, and Mrs. E said firmly, "I promise I will take the medicine right before I go to therapy, and I will get the folks there to tell you that I kept my word." From that day on, Elizabeth took her medicine at the time when it would accomplish its purpose: to help ease the pain of rehabilitating her leg and her hip so she could walk again.

And she was determined to walk. In fact, one day Mrs. Crunk called a friend and asked for his help. "I want you to take my tractor to get an extra step welded on it," she explained, "so I'll be able to drive it when I come home." He didn't take her seriously—and that is a dangerous mistake.

A few days later she called him to check on the progress of the step. When she found out he had not taken in the tractor, Elizabeth reiterated: "I told you to take my tractor to get an extra step welded onto it!"

The step did get welded on, Mrs. E did walk again, she did get up on that tractor, using the extra step and her cane, and she is still bush-hogging the pastures and side of the road along her property.

A WORD ABOUT OUR LAND

As I listened to Mrs. Crunk's stories, I looked at her beautiful vegetable garden containing no weeds and her flower beds covered with mulch from thirty-pound bags she herself loaded onto the cart behind her John Deere lawn mower and then unloaded and spread by herself. I observed how much work she still gets accomplished just five months shy of her ninetieth birthday without complaining about the constant pain or the aggravating need for a cane.

A week ago Mrs. E arrived at my house at 9:00 a.m., helped me pick green beans, string them, and snap them, and then, until 6:00 p.m., she taught two friends and me how to can. We put up six quarts of beans and fourteen quarts of tomatoes. I took her some beans yesterday so she could eat them. When I went to her house today at 4:30, she had just finished canning them for me.

For decades now, Mrs. Crunk has taken seriously the responsibility of caring for the land that she inherited from her father's estate and the acres of her own farm. When I asked her what she would like to say to the next generation about being good stewards of the earth, Mrs. E said, "One of the reasons I signed over my acreage to be protected was that I have headwaters that go to the Duck River. If this land were developed, it would erode, making big ditches and washing dirt to the river. We have to care for the land, but you don't find very many people today who will. If farmers keep using commercial fertilizer, it will kill the earthworms and the microorganisms that enrich the soil and enable plants to grow. It will get to where nothing will grow without that commercial fertilizer."

Mrs. Crunk continued: "We also have to put organic matter back into the soil. We can sow crimson clover or rye or buckwheat (which is great for a garden). If we stop growing our food and raising animals for meat, who do you think will feed us? I don't believe many people today even think about these things, but they should. I think times are going to get even harder, and people will regret the loss of thousands and thousands of acres of farmland that were destroyed so that houses and stores could be built. It's not too late, though. There is still time to take care of the land God has given us."

THE STORIES I KEEP

My friend Karen Fentress, the poet who wrote "A Tale of Peas" at this book's beginning, introduced me to the writings of Wendell Berry, an essayist, novelist, and poet who has a great passion for restoring and preserving small farms and the small-farm way of life. In a collection of essays entitled *The Way of Ignorance*, Berry quotes from a book called *Feed My Sheep* by Terry Cummins. I believe the following passage is a beautiful and accurate description of Mrs. Elizabeth McCord Crunk:

> When you see that you're making the other things feel good, it gives you a good feeling, too … It doesn't seem that taking sweat-soaked harnesses off tired, hot horses would be something that would make you notice.

Opening a barn door for the sheep standing out in a cold rain, or throwing a few grains of corn to the chickens are small things, but these little things begin to add up in you, and you can begin to understand that you're important. You may not be real important like people who do great things that you read about in the newspaper, but you begin to feel that you're important to all the life around you. Nobody else knows or cares too much about what you do, but if you get a good feeling inside about what you do, then it doesn't matter if nobody else knows. I do think about myself a lot when I'm alone way back on the place bringing in the cows or sitting on a mowing machine all day. But when I start thinking about how our animals and crops and fields and woods and gardens sort of all fit together, then I get that good feeling inside and don't worry too much about what will happen to me.[1]

This fits Mrs. E to a "T."

And Mrs. E just couldn't believe that I wanted in this collection some of the stories she had kept and shared with me. But she came around after I told her again and again how important she has been to sustaining and perpetuating life around her—and how she is doing that for me, not only with her depth of knowledge and wisdom, but also by her willingness to spend time with a middle-aged woman who has a great deal to learn about farming and about life.

It is my sincere prayer that someone reading Mrs. E's story will be encouraged to preserve the land, to grow crops, and to raise farm animals. After all, when hard, lean times come back around to the citizens of this nation, *whom will they call?*

They'll call farmers. They'll call folks like Elizabeth Crunk and Mr. Matlock who leases her land for his cattle and cares for the small herd she has—and like me one day. Maybe. These farmers are the salt of the earth at a time when America is losing the flavor of independence and fierce pride.

God, please bless the farmers and their family farms and all the people who work hard to help keep this country and her citizens great. Help all of us love the dirt as well as those folks who live on it and care for it. Bless Mrs. E and Mr. Matlock and all the other local farms in Williamson County.

And show all of us, I pray, the stories we are to keep in order to remember where we have been, so we can know where we are, and know where we need to be going—and so that we can also remember that You have been with us and will be with us every step of the way. Amen.

Pass the salt, please.

The Stories I Keep

END NOTES

Introduction
1. Karen Ann Fentress. "A Tale of Peas," used by permission.

Chapter 1
1. Wendell Berry, "Renewing Husbandry" in *The Way of Ignorance: And Other Essays* (Berkeley, CA: Shoemaker & Hoard, 2006), 95.

Chapter 3
1. Roy Rogers, "The Cowboys' Prayer." Used by permission of The Roy Rogers-Dale Evans Museum in Branson, MO.
2. ———, "Roy Rogers Riders' Club Rules." Used by permission of The Roy Rogers-Dale Evans Museum in Branson, MO.
3. ———, "Sign Off for Radio and Personal Appearances." Used by permission of The Roy Rogers-Dale Evans Museum in Branson, MO

Chapter 5
1. Harper Lee, *To Kill a Mockingbird* (New York: Lippincott, 1960), 294.

Chapter 7
1. James Russell Miller, *Things to Live For* (New York: Thomas Crowell, 1896), 6.

Chapter 12
1. "Just Whittlin'," *The Fayette Chronicle*, April 18, 1970.

❦ END NOTES ❧

Chapter 13

    1. Oswald Chambers, *My Utmost for His Highest* (New York: Dodd, Mead & Company, 1935), 215.

Chapter 15

    1. Mrs. Charles E. Cowman with James Reimann, *Streams in the Desert: 366 Daily Devotional Readings* (Grand Rapids, MI: Zondervan, 1997), 330.

    2. Oswald Chambers, *My Utmost for His Highest* (New York: Dodd, Mead & Company, 1935), 321.

Chapter 16

    1. Terry Cummins, *Feed My Sheep* (Bloomington, IN: 1st Books Library, 2003), 47.

❧ ACKNOWLEDGMENTS ❧

There are many people to whom I owe a debt of gratitude in connection with this book: Jim Stewart, Lana Shealy, and Sonua Bohannon of Xyzzy Press—for taking a chance on me and then guiding this little craft into port; my editor, Lisa Guest—for not sending a hit squad from California to Tennessee—and then making the whole thing work; and all the folks at Birdsong Creative—wow, you are *really* good.

Linda Malone—you were the first to be excited about these stories and even gave me hope; Carolyn Baker, Laura Lyn Donahue, Melinda Seibert—I am grateful for your being present, funny, and honest; Robert Trent—I'm not sure how you have believed in me all these years, but the book is finally *real*; Shirley Green and Karen Fentress—two writers who cheered me on (*your* books are next!); the folks at Fellowship Bible Church in Brentwood, Tennessee; my sister, Sherry Coleman—thanks for checking up on me; and the women who are my heroes and guides—Momma, Nannie, Miss Helen, Mom Walker, Mrs. Elizabeth Crunk, Olice Machen, Polly Powell, Eleanor Kerns, Margaret Hodges McClain, Ruth Graham, and Carol Kent.

To Catelyn, Cami, and Carly Norman; Miss Audrey Ney; Maddie Fowler; and all my younger friends who will carry on long after I am gone—you can trust in Jesus for He will never fail you. Remember: God cares even about red ballet slippers—Can you beat that!

I could not have accomplished this wrenching, writing process without my extraordinary friend and co-"heart" in daily life, Valerie Kagan. You encouraged my weary soul, cooked meals, cleaned my house, kept Miss Millie, planted tomato plants, weeded a wee bit, and protected my sequestered state. You have been the best darn friend I have ever had. Here it is, V—no one is more surprised than I am. Shoot Fire!

Final Word: Jesus is the only reason I am alive and well. Because of God, I can agree with James Taylor, the songwriter and singer: "Unconditional love on a daily basis can melt a stone." I look forward to such fluidity.

To all my "people": Next year in Jerusalem!

RoseAnne's Nannie, Dora Marie Jones Bibles, working in the
Huntsville Manufacturing Company (formerly Merrimack
Textile Mill) in Huntsville, Alabama.

RoseAnne's baby sister, Sherry, with her red cowboy boots and hat on Christmas morning.

RoseAnne before that fateful first day of school where she met Shelia and eventually shared her broken colors.

Tricia Walker's mother Marie Walker and her
"other mother" Jannie Hall.
Courtesy of Tricia Walker, bigfrontporch.com

RoseAnne with her mother, Mary Melrose Bibles Coleman,
and her beloved dog Punkin.

Miss Helen Wright enjoying life!

RoseAnne's life on " a new, sparkling course." She wore
this jacket and jewels the night she met Roy Rogers.
Photo by L. Rutherford Photography